March 28, 2016
To Pam + Jim
It's fun
grand
Love,
June M

M000238272

May's Story

BY

June Morse

the Peppertree Press
Sarasota, Florida

Copyright © June Morse, 2014

All rights reserved. Published by the Peppertree Press, LLC.
the Peppertree Press and associated logos are trademarks of
the Peppertree Press, LLC.

No part of this publication may be reproduced, stored in a retrieval system,
transmitted in any form or by any means, electronic, mechanical, photocopying,
recording, or otherwise, without prior written permission of the publisher and
author/illustrator. Graphic design by Rebecca Barbier.
Cover art by June Morse.

For information regarding permission,
call 941-922-2662 or contact us at our website:
www.peppertreepublishing.com or write to:
the Peppertree Press, LLC.
Attention: Publisher
1269 First Street, Suite 7
Sarasota, Florida 34236

ISBN: 978-1-61493-312-0

Library of Congress Number: 2014920892

Printed in the U.S.A.

Printed December 2014

To all the pioneer women who tried their
best to make a home for their families

Sample of May's Letters

start out for yourself? We have
talked some of trying Oregon or Washington, but I am not willing to go
farther west. I like Colorado and
don't believe we shall ever find
a country that has fewer drawbacks than this. For the last year
we have not made anything on
account of grasshoppers, but I guess
we will rent a ranch next year
and try it again. When we can
get about twenty good dairy cows,
we can do well to move into the
mountains and give up farming.
Here we have a healthy climate
and scenery that can not be excelled
elsewhere, and when grasshoppers do
not come, farmers can raise better
crops and get a better price than
in any of the eastern States.
    Alice was down here two
weeks ago. She has another little
boy nearly two months old now.

Preface

May's Story is written in the letters that May wrote to her family. She was a pioneer woman who traveled to Colorado in a covered wagon, fought the grasshoppers with her husband, took the new Pacific railroad line to California, and had seven children. As a teacher, her letters were beautifully written with descriptions that can't be surpassed. May's life unfolded fraught with many challenges to overcome. It was a time of fundamental Christian belief and moral courage. Through it all she prevailed as the heroine. May was my Great-grandmother.

May's letters were sent to me by Aunt Mable Stanhope who was circulating them around the family. I was a mother with three young children at the time and very busy. I did read the letters and figured out how many children May had. Fifty years later I do have the time, and it was the right time to piece together May's story. Although May was an extraordinary person, she was one of many who went west and faced all odds of making a living. Those strong men and women who had a dream and worked hard trying to live off the land were the expansion of the United States.

I gleaned additional information from the writings of May's son Ed Lyman Jr. and her sister Alice who both had written a short version of May's life. Ed Jr. had also typed his mothers letters in 1913 to have something that would last instead of the fading ink of her letters. There were many letters, but there are many missing. My daughter Evangelyn and I filled in the spaces and decided what might have happened. Therefore, the story is based on truth, but some of it is romantic fiction.

It seemed that May was hungry for her own place, a home for her family. But she is continually moving from place to place as she did when she was a child. After everything is taken away from her she accepts what she can, and makes the best of it to raise her children. Through it all it is God she relies on and in the end has the promised heavenly home. One must read May's letters carefully because they convey the innermost soul of her being, and of women's thoughts of that period of time.

I want to thank my daughter Evangelyn for doing the background digging and helping to write some of the areas that weren't covered by the letters. I am grateful to my husband Tom who worked tirelessly on the computer organizing the letters with the story and putting it in the proper format. My son Tavis helped when the computer didn't do what he wanted.

We got involved with the history and the places that May lived. A trip to Longmont Colorado was enjoyed by Tom, Evangelyn, and myself as we dug through the microfiche at the library, read the old newspapers, and discovered there was a fire that took all the records of the people living there. We went to Estes Park and saw the mountains that were enjoyed by more settlers coming to the area by train.

Tom and I went to Portland to see the Willamette River and the towns where Ed and May lived. We saw the bay front at Newport and the beautiful Nye beach that brought so many tourists to the area in the early 1900's. I imagined the little cottage at Yaquina City where May spent her last days with her family. This has been an adventure to relive the life of the times through May's Letters.

She calls him Lawrence. She said she was going to write to you and Ma soon. She and her family are going with us on our trip to the mountains. I was much disappointed in not receiving a picture of Ma and Cora in your last letter. I do want to see how Ma looks so much. Perhaps in my next letter I will send pictures of my family as I want to have them taken soon.

Give my love to Nettie and Dora every time you see them. Please write to me Jim and tell me all about yourself and all the family and friends. As ever I remain

Your loving Sister

Mary G Lyman.

St Vrain, Weld Co. Colo

List of Letters

Contents

List of Illustrations

John Rhubottom + Elizabeth Harding
Emigrated from England to America – 1774
Settled East bank of the Hudson River

William   Joseph   John Rhubottom
Washington Co. NY
m. Martha B. Allen

Allen   Lawrence   William   Rensselaer
b. 1809   b. 1810   b. 1814   b. Dec. 18, 1816
              m. 1838   m. May 19, 1844
         Orphy Connor   Mary H. Olney
                                         b. Nov. 5, 1822 NY
Nancy Olney   3 other sisters   d. 1850 Medina, MI
b. 1818 NY   d. 1850 La Grange, IN
m. 1840 Hiram Stimson

Eugene   Almeda   Katie
                  b. 1848 NY
                  m. Orson Kent

Mattie   Fannie   Loren (twins) Richard
b. 1866 b. 1867 b. 1872   b. 1872
                  d. 1873

Alice   Rensselaer   Mary (May) Genevieve
b. June 4, 1846   b. July 1, 1848   b. May 26, 1850 Medina MI
m. 1863 Philander Hoyt   m. 1887 Anna   m. May 1870 Kansas
d. Oct. 17, 1867   Edmund Lyman
m. 1872 Isaac Richardson   b. 1845
                                           d. July 29, 1886
Frankie Lawrence Cora   Anna   baby   Summit, OR
b. 1872 Fred   b. Nov5 b. June died
d. 1876 b. May 1875 1877   1880   1883

Johnathan   Edmund   Jessie   Franklin
Fredrick   Rensselaer Jr. May.   Raymond
b. Feb. 3, 1871   b. Jan. 1873   b. Jan. 12, 1875   b. March 20, 1877
Kansas   Longmont CO   Longmont CO   Portland OR

Lawrence   Nancy   Matilda

m. 2nd wife Hannah b.1826

Mary Ann
b.1825

John Warren
b.1830

(Nettie)
Olive Jennett Rhubottom
b.1846 NY
m. Theodore Brown

m. June 7, 1851 Hannah (widow)

Isaac Olney
b.1825
m. Delia E.
b.1824
d.Sept 2, 1867
m.1873 Edwin A Waugh

(Dora)
Francis Rhubottom
(Frank)
b.1858

Hannah Rhubottom
m.1860 La Grange IN
William Painter

Charles
b 1855

Almeda
(Medla)
b.1857
m.1875 OR
Ira Lockhard
b.1840

William
b.1866

Joseph William
(Willie)
b. Aug 1, 1862

Cora Fannie
b. Jan. 17, 1870

Boy
b.1877
d.1880

Jessie
May
b.1879

Florence
b.1881

Edwin
b.1883

Mabel
b.1885

Charles
Henry
b. Feb. 1879
Butteville. OR

Edith F. (Eda)
b. Jan 29, 1881
Yamhill. OR
d. Aug. 14, 1883
Portland OR

Mable Grace
b. June 25, 1885
Hubbard. OR

Rensselaer Rhubottom (father)

Hannah Rhubottom (Painter)

1863
MAY AT UNCLE LAWRENCE'S IN MICHIGAN

"A letter came in the post today for you May, I believe it is from your sister," stated Mrs. Rhubottom, her lips turning in a soft smile, as she reached into her apron and presented a small folded letter. May's face beamed as she eagerly reached for the note. Just one moment before she had been fretting over a careless cut on her finger from the washbasin, and now it was utterly forgotten. She carefully folded her fingers around the note and pressed it to her chest with an inhale.

"And one for Uncle Lawrence as well" Mrs. Rhubottom continued. She turned back to her soup in the kettle without another word. May stood dumbstruck. *Two letters?* She thought. She grabbed the wash basin and ran into the dooryard to toss the spoiled water. Wiping her hands carefully she found her favorite spot beside the flower garden to read her note.

"Alice is to be married!" May shouted running into the kitchen. She nearly tripped over her skirt on the way in the door. Mrs. Rhubottom turned from her soup with wide eyes, "Is she now!" she pondered, " I daresay, so soon!" May could almost see a faint cowl on her lips, as no doubt Mrs. Rhubottom had a notion as to what would happen when Alice left for Battle Creek four months ago.

Mrs. Rhubottom had no children of her own, and May and Alice had both come to her two years hence on the account that May's adopted mother Mrs. Johnson died and her Uncle Lawrence was her nearest relative. May was so distraught, and a tender girl

1

of eleven years, that they sent for Alice, her older sister, to come stay with them.

At first it seemed that Mrs. Rhubottom didn't know quite what to do with two young girls, but she soon realized they were quite capable and she put them to work. "All work is the Lord's work," she would remind the girls, if there was a task that seemed too onerous. She was a taller woman than most and very robust. There was no arguing with Mrs. Rhubottom, and if she got angered, her cheeks would flush red and there would be a hush around the place. At those times it was better to find something out of doors with which to occupy yourself.

Mrs. Rhubottom might have been stern at times, but she was always fair, and she would speak to Uncle Lawrence sweetly and with

Rensselaer Nettie May Alice (1856)

Rensselaer (brother) Mary (May)
Rhubottom

affection. May was glad to have a home, and was a dutiful helper and happy to do her share. It was not like it was with Mrs. Johnson, but now May had Alice, and she meant the world to her. The times she liked best were snuggling up with Alice in the bed they shared and telling stories long into the night.

May was beaming at the news despite Mrs. Rhubottom's lack of enthusiasm. "Get the table set May, your Uncle will be home any moment, and I imagine he will be tired and hungry after drawing stone all day." Mrs. Rhubottom said. May hastily put Alice's letter in her apron pocket and set about putting the plates on the table.

Her Uncles' cabin was small and utilitarian, yet cozy. The log walls were tall enough to afford a small second floor where the two bedrooms were, with two small windows, one on each end of the house. The downstairs was of two rooms, the kitchen and the study with a big stone fireplace set in the middle of both reaching right up through the roof. He had built the cabin himself with help from the neighbors, with logs that were cut off the land. At the time it was the biggest house on the lane, and had the best view of the western fields through its only window in the study.

"Do you think he will read the letter before or after dinner?" asked May with growing anticipation. All she could think about was Alice and her news. Perhaps she was inviting them to attend, or perhaps they were going to plan a visit to Uncle Rhubottoms.

A letter from Alice to Uncle Lawrence could only mean that that some plans were being made.

"Now dear, do calm yourself, he will read it when he is ready and not before," replied Mrs. Rhubottom, set at her task. May sighed and resolved herself to be patient. Before long her Uncle blustered through the door, looking just as tired and worn as Mrs. Rhubottom had anticipated.

"Oh what a day we had today," he breathed as he lowered himself into the chair by the table and took off his hat. His thick strong fingers looked raw, worn and dirty. He pushed them now through his thin grey hair. His eyes were bright and lively however and shone with the same pale blue light as May's. Relatives said he and his younger brother Rensselaer had the same look about the eyes. Their countenance had been similar as well, but May had nothing but a dim recollection of her dear father. He died when she was only six years old, and her mother departed long before then shortly after May was born. May had lived temporarily with the nice Reverend Martin from their church. He was able to secure her with Mr. and Mrs. Johnson, who lived in the village, Mrs. Johnson became her adopted mother until two years ago, when she passed. May's father left a second wife, Hannah, and four children, Alice, Rensselaer, May, and Nettie a daughter from Hannah's former marriage.

May now fidgeted at the table over dinner. "Oh go on, tell him your news May," said Mrs. Rhubottom smiling knowingly.

It was all May needed, "Uncle, I got a letter from Alice and you will never believe it! She is to be married in Battle Creek next month!" she blurted.

Uncle Lawrence abruptly stopped chewing in thought, and then continued musing.

"Well, that was quick, I imagine she means to marry before the regiment musters out. Who is the lucky man?"

May's forehead creased with concern, "She said his name is Philander, the son of William Hoyt the horse doctor."

"Hmm," Uncle Lawrence chewed thoughtfully, "and I expect she might be wanting us to attend?"

"Oh I do hope so Uncle, she also sent you a letter! Pray, please open it! May ventured with the best pleading eyes she could afford under the watchful gaze of Mrs. Rhubottom.

"Now May" she scolded, not unkindly.

"Oh very well, do you have the letter Orphy dear? It seems I must put May out of her misery, before she explodes." Uncle Lawrence declared.

Mrs. Rhubottom produced a small white envelope from her pocket and presented it to Uncle. He took it lightly and turning it round a time or two with a mischievous smile building the anticipation. He then quickly opened it and read slowly with a "hmmmm" here and there for theatrical effect.

At last he folded the letter and declared," Alice has invited all of us to join her for her wedding on Sunday, June 7th. and," he paused and looked directly at May who was beaming, "she requested May to visit as soon as possible. It seems Mr. Hoyt has business in Hudson in a fortnight and he is willing to bring May to Battle Creek on his return." May's eyes went wide and then down at her clasped hands on the table.

"Your Aunt and I will discuss it after dinner" said her uncle, putting an end to conversation and fixing May with a solid gaze.

The remainder of the evening, May washed the evening dishes, wiped the table, and finished her outside chores as dutifully and as quietly as possible thinking her behavior might influence their decision. At last she climbed the ladder to bed and lit the small candle on the chest beside her pillow. She pulled the covers up close, and tucked her long auburn hair into her sleeping cap, and unfolded Alice's letter and read it again.

Dearest May,

You will never guess all the wonderful things that have happened since my last letter. Do you remember Mr. Hoyt's son Philander? He was with Mr. Hoyt when he came to treat Uncles' cow when she wouldn't milk. Well we have become quite fond of each other and, not to delay the news, he has asked me to marry him! It was a shock to me at first as it has only been four months, but I do like him very much. Phil said he did not want to delay with the conscription orders that came this March, Phil will join his regimen in July and he wants us to be wed. Your letters have so cheered me, but now sister I must insist that you visit me in

Battle Creek before my 17th birthday in June, if not before. The Hoyt family is kind and hospitable but I sorely need a comrade to call my own and it would be a blessing for you and Phil to meet before he leaves for his regiment. I have also sent a letter to Uncle Lawrence to invite him and Aunt Orphy and make some possible arrangements for your coming.

Your loving sister, Alice.

May smiled and turned to blow the candle out. They must let her go, she thought. It had been a bitter winter since Alice had left them, as was true of most winters in Michigan, but this one all the more because of Alice's absence. Alice was four years older than May, and May looked up to her keenly. Although Alice and May had been separated from each other when their father died, the past two years together erased all that time between and they were as close as two sisters can be.

At last the morning of her departure came and the sun was just peeking over the dark eastern hills. It was still dark in May's room when she leapt out of bed and shuffled over to where her clothes lay on the chair. She carefully dressed, her cold fingers fumbling over the buttons. Layers of wool and cotton, and the dark green shawl that Mrs. Johnson had given her with a cream embroidery on the edges. It was worn but still sturdy, and May knew that it would be cold in the buggy and it was a long way.

Warm now, she patiently braided her long hair. She had small nimble fingers, but stronger than they looked, much like May herself. She was a slight but sturdy girl, and now that she was thirteen her appetite had grown and she was slimmer than ever, but growing taller in the process. May had noticed that the sleeves of her dress now ended before her wrists and her hem was getting shorter too.

With any luck she and Alice could go fabric shopping in Battle Creek when she arrived. Uncle gave her two dollars for the trip which she kept safely in the pocket of her jacket.

The sun was nearly up by the time May had dressed and packed. She did not have much, but some writing tools, letters, an apron, a picture of Mrs. Johnson, and a pair of extra socks she had stuffed in a pillow case. Aunt Orphy already had the kettle on for oatmeal and she was humming to herself as she scuttled around the kitchen.

If Aunt Orphy was sad that May was leaving, she did not show it. It could have been any other morning. Just then Uncle burst through the door with the milk bucket, nearly sloshing it all over May. She jumped back just in time, but not one drop spilled, and Uncle gave a chuckle at her.

"So you all packed and ready? I imagine Mr. Hoyt will be here soon," he said.

"Yes sir" May replied.

"Well, come have your breakfast" chimed in Aunt Orphy, "and some fresh milk, it's going to be a long ride. I've been up to Battle Creek before and the trip will take you all day until dark if you are lucky, and it will be a long time until dinner."

Just after they finished breakfast they heard a cart approaching outside. May jumped up to get the door.

"Hello in there!" cried Mr. Hoyt as he secured his horses, and made towards the door with a smile. May stepped aside as Uncle Lawrence pushed through the door.

"Good Morning Mr. Hoyt! Good to see you." He greeted Mr. Hoyt with a hearty handshake.

May turned to Aunt Orphy who stood right behind her and gave her a hug. "Thank you so much Aunt Orphy for all your kindness," May gushed squeezing her Aunt tightly. As much as May was excited to see Alice, she did not enjoy leaving. It always seemed as that as soon as she started feeling comfortable in a place, that she would have to say goodbye and start fresh somewhere else.

"Do not fret child, we will see you in Battle Creek for the wedding," Aunt Orphy comforted. "Here, I packed you a lunch of bread and eggs," she said as she handed May a small sack. May thanked her and wiped her eyes. "You tell Alice we will be bringing her favorite peach pie to the wedding. Now go on," and she gave May a little shove towards Mr. Hoyt and Uncle Lawrence.

"Well, well, here is little May," said Mr. Hoyt as he removed his hat and gave a little bow. May smiled and gave a little curtsy in return.

1864
ALICE AND MAY VISIT MOTHER PAINTER

It was wonderful to find themselves at Mother Painters for a visit. Alice and May arrived at La Grange and walked to the house.

After their own mother, whom she was named after, Mary Olney Rhubottom died, their father married Hannah Rhubottom who was the young second widow of grandfather John Rhubottom. It was customary for one of the sons or brothers to marry the widow. Mrs. Rhubottom had one daughter with John named Olive Jennett or "Nettie" as she was called. She was the same age as Alice. When their father died, Hannah Rhubottom was already pregnant with Rensselaer's baby and had a son Francis "Frank." Later Hannah remarried Mr. William Painter and had a son named William "Willie." These were their step sister and brothers.

May and Alice rushed through the porch to give Mother Painter a hug. Alice was very comfortable with her since she had been with her for six years before her father died, and also living with her in La Grange after Hannah had married Mr Painter. Mother Painter was the only mother she knew. But May held back, a bit shy, and not feeling at all like Alice, since Mrs. Johnson had been her adopted mother. May remembered how a couple from N. Y. had wanted to adopt her after Mrs. Johnson died. What a heartache that was living with them. She was so lonesome and upset, she could hardly eat. She had tried to be good, but cried herself to sleep every night. The couple realized what a mistake they had made and sent her back to live with Uncle Lawrence.

Mother Painter put her arms around May.

"How lovely you are here, May, I've always felt like I lost you somewhere. Please feel at home here. You and Alice can stay as long as you like," welcomed Mother Painter. May's heart warmed, Mother Painter had thought of her.

"Thank you very much," May breathed. "It's been nice to be with Alice in her time of need. Alice couldn't wait to come back home to visit you." May looked at Alice hoping she hadn't said too much.

May wondered if it was alright to talk about Alice's emotional depression. When May returned to Alice in February after her four month visit with Aunt Nancy Stimson in N.Y., she expected to help her with a baby in March. Sadly the baby boy passed on to a heavenly place leaving Alice crushed and exhausted. May had helped her through the burial, but it left Alice with an empty heart. Mr. Hoyt had to return to the regiment right away which didn't help matters any.

Alice took both their arms and marched into the kitchen. "Let's have some lemonade and not talk of sad things." She gazed around the kitchen, the same wood stove was centered at the far wall. Even though it was summer it made the room feel warmer.

"I like your new ruffled curtains, Mother." Alice remarked, spying something new.

"Yes, I thought the yellow print would be quite cheerful," answered Mother.

Alice helped squeeze the lemons in the heavy squeezer. every push on the handle brought more juice into the pitcher. May added the water, and Mother carefully measured the sugar.

"Let's sit on the porch," Mother said as she filled three glasses. "We'll take your bags up later. Willie is still napping. I expect Nettie shortly, she went on some errands," she explained, "and Frankie is at school." It was a bright afternoon and the three were in deep conversation sitting on the shaded porch by the time Nettie arrived.

She carried a basket of cheese, eggs, bacon, and fresh bread. Putting it down, Nettie gave each of her sisters a hug.

"Have you been here long? How was your trip? It seems like ages since I've seen you, but it was just last year at Alice's wedding." Nettie moved another chair closer and sat down.

"Let me get you some lemonade," offered May.

"Thank you, I would love some," Nettie answered.

Alice asked, "what do you think you'll do now that you're through school?"

"I'm not sure, I have no beau yet, and I would hate to get a job that I don't like; I was thinking of teaching," Nettie smiled.

"That is a satisfying profession, educating the children," May agreed handing her a glass of lemonade.

"There's the Seminary in Wilksville that you could get your teaching certificate," advised Mother Painter.

"That would take a few years, wouldn't it?" asked Nettie.

"I think you can take classes all year there. It would probably take two years at least. It's so near here you could stay at home," Mother added.

"What about you May, it seems like you would like to be a teacher too," claimed Nettie.

"I haven't even finished school yet, I keep missing when I move from place to place," sighed May.

"That doesn't mean that you couldn't catch up," Alice told her. "I'm sure the sisters at the seminary would teach you what you need to know at whatever level you start. Isn't that right Nettie?"

"Why don't we do it, May! We could go together and stay here with Mother." Nettie sounded very convincing.

"Well I suppose so," May tentatively agreed. She didn't want to impose on Mother Painter.

"That sounds like the best plan I've heard," exclaimed Mother. "I would love having you stay here, May. Do think about it."

At that point Willie woke up and clambered down the stairs. He spotted his mother on the porch and she lifted him onto her lap. Rubbing his eyes, he pointed at Alice and May. Alice's heart melted, he was the cutest little toddler. May watched and saw Alice's heart-strings being tugged.

"These are your other sisters, Alice and May," introduced Mother Painter. Willie snuggled further into his mother's arms and looked up shyly.

Their attention changed to Frankie who was coming up the porch returning from school. He was in the first grade and was pleased to be able to go to school on his own. As Mother introduced him to May their blue eyes met and immediately she accepted her step brother. He went to her and shook her hand in a manly way which impressed May for such a young child. Surely she could stay here and be part of the family and finish her education.

In the evening preparing supper, the three sisters helped Mother Painter with Frankie setting the table. Mr. Painter arrived home and met May. They all sat at the table and Mr. Painter said the Grace. Then they discussed the new plans for Nettie and May.

"It may be too late for the summer courses," Mother Painter pointed out, "but in September they shall start again."

"Will there be a test before registration to decide what classes would be best?" asked May.

"We shall go next Monday to find out what we need to do," said Nettie.

"Let's go on a picnic Saturday at the lake," suggested Frankie, thinking of a swim. He had directed his inquiries to Mr. Painter.

"Well, I'm sure we could arrange that," his father nodded. He was proud of Frankie although Willie was the apple of his eye.

"I'll cook up some chicken and Nettie shall bake a blueberry pie. She picked enough blueberries yesterday." Mother Painter looked around the table at the children's eager faces. Alice was already feeling much better being back with the family.

"We would like to help too! Please put us to work!" begged Alice.

"There shall be lots to pack in the wagon," replied Mother. "We'll start preparing in the morning and be ready for Saturday's picnic."

"Don't forget, after Saturday's outing, Sunday we shall all attend church. That's the Lord's day, a day of rest." Mr. Painter warned them. He knew how tired they would be and he always looked forward to his nap on Sunday afternoon.

The day dawned clear and hot. They loaded the wagon and the ladies made sure they had parasols and blankets. The lake was several miles away and May looked forward to swimming with the heat of the day coming on. Soon enough they were spreading the blankets on the grass and changing into bathing outfits. There was a game of horse-shoes going on and other families were gathered around the beach area. Mr. Painter started resting right away while the others enjoyed the water. Mother Painter had Willie digging in the sand. He managed to smash every mound she built up. May and Alice played with him too, digging holes and watching the water filling them up. May could hardly believe this was her life ahead of her for the next two years. She had a family to live with, brothers and sisters. It was like soaking in love and acceptance.

1868
MAY'S STAY WITH AUNT DELIA

May was content to sit in the carriage and let the cold breeze settle the dust from the horses on the leather seat. She was glad to get away from her teaching duties and visit Aunt Delia who was married to her mother Mary Olney's brother Isaac. It would be a busy time for Aunt Delia since Uncle Isaac had died and left the newspaper business to run. She was running the *Garnett Plaindealer* with her two children and probably wouldn't have much time for visiting.

It was one of the first sunny warm days they'd had since the cold winter and May turned her face up to feel the feeble warmth of the afternoon sun. The clouds were rapidly casting a shadow over the dry earth of Garnett Co. Kansas. The land stretched out on either side of the carriage, dry brown fields to the horizon waiting to be planted. Despite the bleak landscape, Garnett boasted of a bustling new town, flush with the promise of a new railroad stop. Surely Garnett would become a hub of commerce and development. May also hoped there would be an open teaching position, she did not want to depend on Aunt Delia, and in no way wanted to be a burden. If everything went well, she would be able to pay her keep, and help Aunt Delia with the paper and her family as well.

With all her teaching experience, she was confident she could make a place for herself. She planned to be fully settled by her next birthday May 26, 1868 when she would be 18.

May had reservations leaving poor Alice whom she had left grieving over the death of her husband, Mr. Philander Hoyt. (He had been in the army as an assistant surgeon stationed at Grand Rapids 6th Michigan Heavy Artillery and returned from the war two years ago. His bowel trouble had lead to tuberculosis and he died in the fall.)

Soon the fields fell away and the buildings of downtown Garnett, Kansas came into view. Before long the carriage pulled into the center of town. Indeed, Garnett was full of activity, carriages and horses in the dusty street. Local merchants and people busy purchasing wares, and children darting in and out of the carts.

Aunt Delia came out of the *Garnett Plaindealer's* office to greet her as the carriage pulled to a stop. "How are you May Genevieve?" she called.

May stepped down from the carriage and hugged her aunt. "I am fine, it was a pleasant ride, thank you Aunt Delia," May replied.

"Do bring your things in the house and get settled." Delia said as she opened the door to her house next to the office.

"How kind of you to have me when you're so busy with the newspaper," murmured May.

"It's no trouble at all, I've been waiting to see you now that you're grown up, and I daresay that you will be more of a comfort to me than anyone I have had in a while." They made their way through the front parlor and up the stairs to the three bedrooms.

"Now Media is staying with me in my room," explained Aunt Delia, "and Charles and Willie are in the room across the hall." She shuffled quietly through the hallway, and then whispered," Willie is having his nap now. Here is the back bedroom; it has a nice view over the back fields and gets a lot of sunlight," she smiled and opened the door.

May was immediately put at ease, the room was small, but clean and bright with a sitting chair and desk by the window. "Oh this is lovely, thank you!" May breathed. She set down her case and took off her coat and hat. She felt at home immediately.

"Now come down for some hot tea when you are ready," said Aunt Delia," I need to catch up on what's going on with you and Alice."

They sat at the table in the kitchen while Aunt Delia poured two cups of black tea. May described Alice's plight. "After Mr. Hoyt died, Alice and I went to visit Aunt Nancy Stimson, your sister-in-law. They had moved from their wealthy home in New York to Ottawa, Kansas, to be missionaries to the Indians under the Baptists. They have a nice little home there. Their daughter Katie was visiting and invited Alice to stay with them. Katie and Mr. Kent have two little girls and could use some help."

"That's wonderful for Alice, it will keep her busy and not thinking so much about her troubles," Aunt Delia exclaimed. "Now what about all of your teaching, May?" she asked.

"Well, you know I went to the Seminary with Nettie in Wilksville near LaGrange, Indiana in 1864" May started in. "It was so close to Mother Painter's that when we talked of it, it made perfect sense to become a teacher. We graduated in less than two years and my first school was in the Haw Patch five miles south from LaGrange. I taught there two terms."

"Oh, and what is the Haw Patch, it sounds dreadful" Aunt Delia asked.

"It's actually a fertile plain with sugar maples and black walnut trees. It was named the Haw Patch because of the abundance of hawthorns trees that grow there," stated May.

She continued on. "Then I went to Missouri where Alice was living at Carrollton. Her husband Mr. Hoyt had returned from the army and was elected County School Superintendant. I received my teaching certificate and started teaching a darky school. But the slavery people made so much objection that the darky schools were discontinued."

At this time in history the blacks had just gained their independence through the civil war and the passage of the 14th amendment. But life was hard for them in the states that were in between. Even though the federal law stated that blacks were free, there were sentiments on either side of the aisle. A federal movement was made to establish schools for black children, but most of the funding came from the states, so they pretty much underfunded the schools to the point of disrepair. Most schools were nothing more than a broken down building, no heat, sometimes broken windows, and certainly no supplies or books. Attendance was spotty at best. Most kids had a hard time coming regularly because they needed to work for the family, or they were constantly sick or simply did not have the means and supplies.

May then got a break with her brother in-law at his school, but he was largely unpopular in the town because he was in the army and likely did not share their views on slavery. Regardless, he died of tuberculosis he caught while in the war.

Helping herself to more tea, May was urged on by Aunt Delia, "What did you do then?" she asked.

"I took a school for white children about eight miles south of Carrollton on the river bottom. It was difficult and Mr. Hoyt helped me to get a good school across the river in Saline Co. I taught there until Mr. Hoyt died. The whole school system was taken over since there were bitter feelings against him." May noticed that Aunt Delia looked tired.

"I hope I haven't tired you, Aunt Delia, let me get supper while you rest," May insisted.

"I have a stew on the stove, thank you May for offering," said Aunt Delia. "I need to run next door and close the office; Charles and Media were minding it for a bit."

May enjoyed the family at supper and noted how grown up Media seemed at eleven years old. Charles at thirteen was playing with Willie who was two-years old.

Upstairs in her bedroom, May thought about her step mother Hannah Painter. She had been so gracious in giving her a home while studying with Nettie. Now May felt that she had a mother, someone to confide in and help guide her. She had a chance to get to know Frankie and Willie as brothers. Nettie had a steady beau and they were to be married. Teaching had matured May. She realized Mother Painter had her own family to care for. May longed for a place to call home after shuffling from one family or relative to another. Finally sleep overcame her and May dreamed of her own home.

The winter went by slowly. May had found a teaching position in Garnett which kept her mind occupied. Living with Aunt Delia was convenient and she could tell Aunt Delia liked having her there and kept urging her to learn to set type. (Charles was helping his mother after school at the newspaper.) A letter from Alice arrived and May devoured every word.

MAY'S LETTER TO MOTHER PAINTER, FEB. 16, 1868

Garnett, Kan. Feb. 16, 1868

My own dear mother.

Your letter reached me about two hours ago and I feel like writing so will answer immediately although I have no news to send. I was so very glad to know that I was not forgotten in that dear old home. And how much I would give to be with you today-this lovely Sabbath morning. How much I want to tell you that can not be said with pen and paper. I am seated up stairs in my open window and all around me is beauty but I do not feel in a humor to enjoy anything. The sun is shining warm and there is not a breath of air stirring. We have had no rain here for over three months and everything is dry and parched up. We have had some quite cold weather and it has snowed once or twice but only a very little. I never dreamed that Kansas was so very different from Indiana. My health has been very good all winter and I am strong as I ever was in my life. My winter term of school will close next Friday but I shall take a contract for another month and keep right on and then engage four months' summer school so that I shall have no vacation at all. Alice is in Burlington, Coffee Co., Kan., about 25 miles west of me on the Neosho river. I had a letter from her this morning and she said she was coming up to see me this week and wanted me to be ready to go back home with her. I shall be glad to see her but cannot go away with her as I can not leave my work. A teacher is always tied down too closely to allow time for much pleasure.

Poor Alice, you spoke truly in saying that she had a full share of trouble in this world. But still she always has the faculty of throwing off trouble and enjoying herself in spite of fate. She is now with our cousin in Burlington and seems to like it first rate. There she can go in the best society and Kate has a nice home, plenty to make anyone happy. I had a letter from Nettie not long ago and was glad to hear that she was so well satisfied with her lot in life. If I ever marry I could not be contented to settle in the west for I cannot feel "at home" here. But Kansas is a noble state and I believe that in ten years it will be fully equal to any in the Union. The cars will run through this town by the fourth of July next and then we will be as well calculated for business prosperity as anyone. I am intending to have some photographs taken this Spring and will send you one. I want to wait until my 18th birthday so that I may always know just how I looked then. And now I must close. This has been a long letter and there is not much in it but it helps me to spend some of the time. Please write to me soon and often and let me know how you are prospering. I will write as often as I can and tell you if I change places so you may know all the time where I am. Leaving all to the keeping of our Father let us trust in Him and hope to meet again.

Yours as ever,

May

ALICE'S LETTER TO NETTIE & THEODORE, FEB. 16, 1868

*Care of Orson Kent, Burlington Coffee Co.,
Kansas. Feb. 16, 1868.*

Dear lost sister and brother.

I had long since given up as lost supposing we were not worthy of correspondence -but last evening I received a letter from darling May and enclosed was one from you asking me to write if I thought you "worthy of correspondence." Nettie how can you say that when I have written so many, many times and no answer from home for nearly a year-for shame. Well, Nettie this is all the paper I could find so I must make the best of it-perhaps you think we are out of the world but we are just in it. I like it out here very much indeed. Because I am among my own mother's relatives and they are truer than Pa's.

I now make my home with cousin Katie, Aunt Nancy's daughter, she is only nine months older than I and is married to a very wealthy New Hampshire man, Orson Kent by name. They have two little girls, Mattie 22 months and Fannie 7 months and this you know suits me. This is a very happy family and I am very well contented and I would be happy if sister May was with me. She is 30 miles from here staying with Aunt Delia, Uncle Isaac's widow. Katie has a large piano and organ and at times will make the house ring, but dear sister with all my pleasures of western life you and my dear mother are thought of daily- and many tears have been shed to think you had forgotten me entirely, or had discharged

21

us out of the home circle. I never appreciated Ma so much in my life as I have since I have had so much trouble. Perhaps you have heard all about it, I will not attempt to describe it as it would take volumes to commence with, but suffice to say I am left a widow, alone and childless but it is better that I am for my married life has been full of trials-and now I am at leisure to go just where I can do best and my objects now to teach here or in Franklin County, this state, and next Fall go back to Missouri in the southern part, and teach there as long as I stay in the west, and when I am 25 and have made my fortune I am coming to see you and my old home. How wisely you have been to settle down there and stay, how much better it would have been if we had done the same, but that is all in the past. Do for mercy's sake tell me how La Grange looks, where is your house and where has it improved and how, who are still living that I knew and who lives in our home, where is Ma and how is she. Is darling little Frankie almost a man, don't let him forget me and Nettie, among our misfortunes, we have lost every picture, books, photographs, and everything that belonged to the family and even Pa's Masonic and Hymn book all have gone, and now I want Ma's and Frankie yours and Dora's and don't forget it either. I have not a picture to my name. Tell Dora he will surely spoil you if he goes to cooking, but while he is about it to save a grand old dish of oysters for me for I am very fond of them. I attended an oyster supper and dance new years eve in Ottawa and had such a good time but did not get introduced to a "Husband". "Dora I am coming back there sometime to have you try that over again. Nettie, I don't care if my paper is dirty, accept it.

From Alice Hoyt

NED

Something happened that unraveled May.

Aunt Delia came in after closing the office. "May, I'm glad you're here." she started, "a gentleman from Hudson Michigan. came by looking for you. His name is Ned Haskins."

"What! I haven't seen him since I was a child and we lived with Mrs. Johnson. She took him in the same time that I went to live with her." reasoned May.

"He said he would come later to see you, so be warned" replied Aunt Delia.

After supper May cleaned the kitchen and freshened up expecting Ned. Soon a knock on the door brought her face to face with the boy she had known for several years.

"May, I hope you remember me. I apologize for surprising you, but I couldn't get you out of my mind and I had to find you and see you. How are you?" spluttered Ned.

"I am well, thank you. Why didn't you write to me and let me know that you might visit?" she asked walking out to the porch.

"I didn't know how you would take this visit and I had to see you in person," Ned answered wiping his brow.

"It is nice to see you. How are you doing back home?" May inquired.

"I'm a teacher now at the academy in Hudson. I have a house near the school. I've been thinking of you and how we both were thrown together when we were young and homeless. Now that we're both older and I have a home well..." he hesitated. "I always looked at you as an angel and admired your character and grace. All these years you have been the angel of my heart and I hoped that you would come home with me to become my wife. Please marry me, May, my angel?" Ned looked at May closely to see her reaction.

May was so surprised that it took a moment to collect her thoughts. "Ned, I think fondly of you as a brother, never in my mind has that changed. We were bound by a need of a home as children, but now I cannot consent when my heart doesn't feel as you do." May exhaled slowly hoping she hadn't hurt Ned too drastically. "Now that you have a successful position surely you will find someone to fulfill your angel dream in truth instead of fantasy," she finished.

Ned was pale and eyed her soulfully "I guess I've been chasing a dream and I'm sorry if I've offended you." He looked like a wounded puppy and May felt sad for deflating him.

"Before you go back please come tomorrow for tea and meet Aunt Delia and the children. I truly would like to hear how everyone is back in Hudson," offered May.

"Alright," gulped Ned. "I might as well visit if you can forgive me for assuming that you would have similar feelings."

"Forgiven," May nodded. "I do like you as a friend. Now that is straightened out I will see you tomorrow." May turned and went inside to her room.

How strange it was to have someone offering her a home and she couldn't even think of it. She would never feel the same way that Ned was. God wouldn't allow a relationship based on false feelings. May listened to her heart and shook off any doubt. She thought about how sad it was when Mrs. Johnson died. That was when May went to live with Uncle Lawrence Rhubottom until a wealthy family in New York wished to adopt her. She went with them and they treated her very kindly, provided her with everything. But being a very sensitive and reserved young child, she became homesick and returned to Uncle Lawrence in Michigan.

She loved living and traveling with Alice, and now she was with Aunt Delia. May knew she wanted her own home, but she had to follow her true feelings.

The next day went smoothly and Ned enjoyed the little family in spite of how he felt about May. He told her how Mr. Johnson was and that he sent his regards. The whole trip was very different than what he expected. May and he parted friends. May thanked God for the strength to stand up for herself and she sighed with relief after Ned had left.

THE SECOND TEMPTATION

May was busy with the *Plaindealer* and helping Aunt Delia all summer. September came and with it the school classes. May was eager to start the students off with reading and writing assignments. she loved correcting their English and seeing where their imaginations let them travel. The only duties she had for Aunt Delia was setting type on the weekend and taking the deposits to the bank.

As she stepped off the porch thinking about fitting in some time to help Media and Charles with their school work, she automatically lifted her skirts to cross the muddy street where the rain soaked into the carriage wheel ruts. Her high laced shoes would have to be cleaned and polished again. They had lasted a few years now that her feet had stopped growing. All her clothes had serviced her well over the last year of teaching, but a new Sunday skirt would be nice. She could probably buy some black cotton or even taffeta for sewing a more fashionable skirt. Approaching the bank, May turned her thoughts to the man who worked as the manager. It seemed that he came out of the back office every time she made a deposit; and there he was now.

"How do you do Miss Rhubottom, a fine day after the rain, don't you agree?" He shook her hand making her shift the leather money pouch to her other hand.

"Good day, Mr. Dobson, yes it's wonderful to see the sun again," May replied. She hurried to the counter to make the transaction. He was still waiting at the door.

"I would like to accompany you across the muddy road and help you from tripping over the ruts." Mr. Dobson adjusted his glasses. "You look so lovely today it would be a shame to get mud on your clothes. Besides I have been meaning to talk to you," he continued.

May didn't have a chance to agree or not. He took her elbow and steered her down the stone steps.

"I was thinking how nice it would be to go to dinner at the Inn this Friday. Of course your Aunt Mrs. Olney would be invited too. I have a friend coming into town so it would be the four of us. What do you say Miss Rhubottom, I could use your help in entertaining my friend?" he pressed her arm as she was holding her skirt from a passing wagon.

"Well... I..." May didn't know what to say; she didn't expect this from an older man. How could she refuse. "I'll ask Aunt Delia if she will be able to come," hesitated May. "Thank you, I'll be fine now," as they came to her steps. She extracted herself from his grip and looked at his face. He had a dark mustache and arched eyebrows. She knew he smoked cigars from the smell about him. He tipped his hat to acknowledge her leaving which showed his dark hair receding even though he carefully combed it into place.

Later that night after supper when they were washing dishes, May told Aunt Delia about the invitation.

"It would be good to get out and meet other people," Aunt Delia surmised. Mr. Dobson might be older but he has a good job! Since I'll be there with you, you can get a better idea about who he is without worrying that he might take advantage of you." Delia was watching out for May's interest.

"I guess it would be alright, and I'm very grateful that you will be by my side. What about his friend?"she asked.

"That's fine we can deal with a friend who needs entertaining." she went to tuck in young Willie and left May wondering how the evening would work out. While her thoughts were still turning over in her head, May went to see how Media was doing with her studies.

Friday arrived and May returned from school. She helped Aunt Delia close the office and instruct the two older children to feed Willie and put him to bed. This was the first time they would both be out without the children.

The Inn was busy for a Friday night. Along with Mr. Dobson's friend came other people from the stagecoach. Mr. Dobson introduced his friend Henry Swartz, a business man dressed in a suit. He shook May's and Delia's hand and May couldn't help but notice two big rings on his fingers. She looked at Mr. Dobson's hand and saw a big ring worn on his middle finger. He held the chair for her and they all settled around the table. After telling the waitress their choices of beef stew, chicken and dumplings, or soup and salad, Mr. Dobson talked about the gold claims that had been found out west. While Mr. Swartz talked to Delia about managing a claim for a client, May turned the conversation to Mr. Dobson.

"Where did you live before coming to Garnett?" she asked him.

"I'm from Indiana from a big family and went off on my own while young. I worked at a horse ranch and went into racing horses for a while. The young woman whom I married died in a horse accident and I left horses and went into banking." Mr. Dobson cleared his throat.

"I'm sorry to hear that about your wife, Mr. Dobson," May sympathized. "I'm originally from Michigan, but my step mother

27

lives in Indiana where I finished my education."

"Please call me Richard," he insisted. "You are a fine educated woman whom I admire, May, if you would allow me to call you by your first name. I noticed you when you started to help Mrs. Olney at the newspaper. You are very attractive if you don't mind my saying that." He looked at her white skin, dark hair and light blue eyes. May cringed under his gaze. She didn't feel as if she was getting to know him.

"I'm not used to getting many compliments," she murmured. "How do you like living here in Garnett?" May returned.

"I'm doing well at the bank. The country is growing and people want to keep their money safe. We give loans to the new businesses and invest wisely. There's a lot of construction going on. Now that the war is over, there are more people working and more banks opening."

"Delia interjected, "I hope there is someone interested in buying the Plaindealer who could grow the business. I would like to have more time with my children before they go off on their own." Richard assured her that more people were coming into town every day that would be interested in running the newspaper. Even though Mr. Swartz was just visiting, he knew several businessmen whom he could tell about the *Plaindealer.*

They had finished their dinner and Delia spoke up about getting back home to her children. May and Delia said their good evenings and May agreed to see Richard again on a personal time.

May went with Mr. Dobson to a political rally and another time to a fundraiser dinner.

With the holidays coming he invited her to see his Christmas decorations and have dinner at his house in town. His cook was instructed to serve them and then depart for the evening.

May was pleased to have a Christmas break from school.

Although she loved her students dearly it was a chore to keep ahead of their learning and try to challenge their minds. She was glad to have a chance to do some reading on her own, and then there was Richard Dobson. She wasn't sure what she felt about him. There wasn't an attraction that she felt; it was more like a curiosity about what motivated him.

Nevertheless, she was in good spirits as Richard walked her to his place. The stars were out and they could see their breath in the air. May was grateful to get out of the cold and into the warmth of his house. The table had been moved to make room for a Christmas tree. It was beautifully decorated with colored balls and popcorn. A tiny star was at the top. Richard had the candles lighted in the windows and on the table. He was talking about how beautiful she looked and how lucky he was to have her attentions.

May felt like she was in a dream being played out where she was watching him compliment her and offering her drinks which she declined, even after much pleading about holiday cheer. The dinner was stuffed goose with rice and herbs. She was mesmerized by the scene topped off with special little cupcakes and custard with cream for dessert. Richard was so attentive to her that she felt like a queen.

While she was enjoying herself he gave her a gift, a small rectangular box wrapped in shiny paper. As she carefully opened it she couldn't believe her eyes. It was a gold necklace glowing in the candle light. Richard helped with the clasp and May could smell his breath on her neck. How could she have let this get out of her control! What was happening! Richard was saying things she didn't want to hear.

"Oh no! Richard, this is too expensive, I cannot accept this!" May gasped.

"This is just the beginning, May, I want to lavish you with gold and jewels. You will be the richest lady in town, and you will be mine. I will show everyone in town what an exquisite lady I have and you'll never have to want for anything." Richard looked at her like a trinket he had acquired at the fair, someone to look beautiful next to him.

May reached up and undid the clasp. She held the necklace in her hand seeming to burn the flesh. How could she be so blind. He was buying her love. Her mind cleared in an instant and she knew this was not what she wanted. How many other young girls had been seduced by him. She gathered her wits and tried not to be rude.

"This is too much, I can't possibly accept this or any other expensive gifts. Richard, I don't want to feel beholden to you since I can't truly give my heart." May was slowly backing away and Richard could see that his plan wasn't working with her.

"I don't mean to offend you May. I hoped that you would feel that I could take care of you." He followed her to the door. May was quickly putting on her coat. She let him walk her home since it was late, but her good nights were chilly. Richard could never win her heart.

How had she not seen through his schemes. All that time boasting about being well off and wanting to take care of her. What about the girl he had mentioned, Ellen, who had written him a letter from Indiana which he had quickly wrinkled up and said it was nothing! May tied together her thoughts of Ellen Dodge, an acquaintance from La Grange, Indiana, who had graduated before her. Ellen had left the town to get married and May didn't know where she had settled. May was determined to get to the bottom of this and understand what was going on in his life.

Delia was concerned about May who seemed to be consumed in finding out about Richard's background. She agreed to take the deposits to the bank so May wouldn't have to talk to him.

The rest of the winter May was busy with her students, but by her birthday she chanced to see Richard again. He had the audacity to ask for her hand in marriage thinking that was what she was waiting for. He gave her a month to decide because he wanted to announce the engagement on the fourth of July at the town's festivities.

MAY'S LETTER TO MOTHER MAY 30, 1869 - TEMPTATIONS

Scipio, Anderson Co., Kan. May 30, 1869

My dear Mother.

How many times have I written to you and, as I sealed the letter, would say "This is certainly the last time I will write unless I hear from her soon." But Ma, I am too anxious to hear from you to allow my pride to keep me from begging for one letter. Nettie and Dora manage to write me a letter after I had taken every means in my power to draw one word. From them I learned that you and the children were well. But although I was grateful to learn even that much yet that is not enough. I want a letter right from you, in the dear old familiar hand writing that wrote the first letter I ever received in my life. Mother, I welcome these letters more now than I did then. For as I grow older I learn every year to appreciate your love. Last Wednesday I was nineteen years old. Growing old. My birthday for the last six birthdays have been spent in the school room with the exception of my 15th. And Ma, you know how I am constantly changing homes and going so often among entire strangers to seek a home and friends. But you do not know all the bitter trials and temptations which are all round me and with which I try so hard to battle bravely. Twice within the last year have I been tempted most bitterly. Twice have I seen a nice comfortable home opened for me to enter if I would consent. But I cannot barter myself for a home or for gold when I know my heart could not sanction it. I have never loved anyone well enough to entrust myself to their care and I know it is a sin in the sight of God and my parents to give the hand without the heart. Yet you must know how hard it was for me to turn from home and face again the hard path of duty. God only knows how my heart yearns for a home, some place for rest. But could I ever enjoy my eternal home if I purchased my earthly one at so dear a price? Such thoughts have been sufficient to keep me in duty's path. But how much good at that time would a letter from you have done me. But I excuse your neglect some, knowing it is more of a task for you to write than it is for me. So I keep on writing knowing I can trust you with secrets no one else is in possession of. Now ma, what I want now very much is to get the address of her who once was Ellen Dodge. I heard she had married and moved away but what her name is or where she is, is more than I know. It is quite important that I should know between now and the first of July, sooner if possible. Please Find out if you can and write me just as soon as you can and I will some time tell you all about it. Love to Frankie and Willie and a goodly portion to yourself from your

Loving daughter, May.

When May received her mother's letter she knew exactly what kind of man Mr. Dobson was, a married man who had left his wife and child and now sought after young women who would enhance his image by offering a life of ease and riches. How badly she felt falling prey to his intentions. She was grateful to God for opening her eyes before it was too late. God had guided her through this temptation and she listened with her heart which was never really attracted to this man. She felt no qualms in rejecting his proposal and even mentioned Ellen in her refusal. She wanted him to know that he couldn't fool her anymore.

The newspaper was very busy over the summer with construction news and advertizing products. May squeezed in some time for reading and making her new skirt for Sundays. She was seeing the fashions change from just a gathered skirt to one with a little bustle in the back. She was pleased to find some black taffeta which was somewhat shiny and smooth to the touch. It would go perfectly with the blouse she made last year if she added some lace to the sleeves and neck. May was glad to use Aunt Delia's sewing machine, but she did the lace and the hems by hand. She dismissed the Dobson affair with only the lesson learned. May was looking forward to her life ahead happily helping her Aunt and doing her teaching. Things had a way of working out for the best.

1869
MAY MEETS ED LYMAN

A handsome man in his mid twenties caught May's eyes when he strode into the *Plaindealer's* office one hot afternoon. May was setting type for her Aunt Delia when she looked up to wait on a customer and her attention was taken up by a tall clean shaven man wearing farm clothes with the collar of his blue shirt open. He looked a bit surprised.

"So who is helping at the office now? May I ask?" Ed looked into her light eyes. He hadn't seen this young woman in the office before and couldn't imagine he'd overlooked her. He knew that Isaac Olney the owner of the paper had died two years previously and the widow Delia was running it.

"I'm May Rhubottom," she replied. "I'm helping Aunt Delia. How may I help you" as she avoided his direct gaze.

"I'm Ed Lyman, and I want to run an ad for my father," he said matter of fact. We have a farm ten miles south in Linn County. Here's the information that he wrote out."

"This will come out in the next edition," May assured him and finalized the transaction. His eyes matched his shirt and had a little twinkle in them. She didn't know what to say and commented on the hot weather.

"How would you like to go for a cold lemonade at the cafe after you finish here?" he asked. It would be a shame not to spend a little time with her while he was in town. She looked so sweet and hardworking with an apron on. Her brown hair was pulled up with a few strands hanging down in the heat.

"I can't now until Charlie gets back" she was stalling trying to think of what to say. "Maybe you could come back later and I'll make some lemonade. I have to watch Willie," she motioned to the toddler keeping himself busy with a pair of old boots.

"I'll be back in an hour or so. I'd rather have lemonade that you make anyway," he chuckled. Ed tipped his hat and strode out as easily as he came in. Only now his thoughts were pleasantly on May.

When he returned, May looked neat in a summer white dress and a different apron. She called to him from the porch and Delia was with her. After exchanging pleasantries with Delia and accepting some lemonade he quizzed May and found her quite educated and teaching school in town.

May was curious about him too and saw that he had good manners and a good reputation according to Aunt Delia. As the weeks went by she saw Mr. Lyman quite often under Delia's watchful eye. May was delighted that he didn't drink liquor or swear. He was a hard worker and loved farming.

The Fall slipped past and May was busy with school. The church young people had put together a play depicting the harvest season and giving thanks for their many blessings. Ed had offered to transport the costumes and props in his wagon. He remembered to have a warm blanket to throw over their laps since the weather was colder now. As he picked up May and Delia at the house he pulled the blanket up for them to climb under.

"Oh, This blanket is perfect Mr. Lyman," sighed May. "Media and her friends from the church put these costumes together. They've been rehearsing all afternoon."

"I'm glad the children have been busy with the play," Delia added.

"I'm happy to help out; it gives me more time with you," Ed smiled at May. He reached under the blanket and found her hands and gave them a squeeze. His hands were warm on her chilly fingers. Then he grabbed the reins and gave the horse a 'giddy-up'. It wasn't very far to the church on the other side of town.

Ed helped unload the benches and baskets and set up the table at the end of the hall. May fitted the costumes on the children with Media's instructions. The chairs had been set up and Ed guided Delia to the front row for a seat.

"Delia, I wanted to ask you since you're family to May that I am serious about May and need your permission to court her." Ed kept his voice low.

"Mr. Lyman, of course I approve. May is a lovely girl and you two make a good hardworking couple." Delia answered as she talked into his closest ear.

"Thank you Mrs. Olney," Ed whispered. Now he could pursue his girl in earnest and he smiled to himself.

May joined them and the audience took their seats for the play. They shared pies that had been made for the feast. Thanks for the food was said. An enactment of the pilgrims and Indians coming together went well with only a few prompted lines. Everyone felt the gifts of God's hand work in their lives. The evening came to a close with the song *Blest be the Tie that Binds*.

Ed loaded the benches and props back into the wagon. Delia and May climbed up to the seat with a hand from Ed. Media, Charlie and Willie clambered into the back. They reached the house and took everything inside. May walked Ed out to the porch to thank him and say goodnight.

"You've been so good helping to get things to the church," May told him

"I'm glad to do it," he answered. "It gave me a chance to talk to Delia about courting you. She approved, now do you?" He tilted her head so he could see her eyes.

"You're the only one I've been seeing Ed." She looked down so he couldn't read anymore from her eyes.

"I'd like to ask you to the Christmas Church dinner next month. I know it's early, but I'm going to be away for a couple of weeks and I want to make sure you'll go with me as my girl." He put his finger under her chin and bent to kiss her. May didn't resist. She closed her eyes and felt a warm tingling sensation go through her. Her arms went around his neck and she was pulled closer until their bodies touched in a full hug.

She managed to whisper in his ear "I'll miss you until I see you again."

He stroked her soft cheek. "It will go by fast and Christmas will be here." He kissed the end of her nose and then her warm lips.

May wondered where Ed was going for two weeks. He had already invited her to meet his parents at the farm on Christmas so she looked forward to the holidays and the visit. Her mind was busy with getting through the school session especially since she was working at the newspaper office setting type after school and didn't have much time to go over the children's lessons.

Meanwhile Ed had secured a ride with his friend to go into Kansas City to do some shopping and to meet someone his father knew who had worked on the farm His friend lived nearby and was engaged to be married. They both needed to find a special present for their women. When this was done Ed could relax and know that he was prepared for the Christmas holiday. He couldn't wait to get together with May again and enjoy this special season.

Christmas morning Delia and Media and Charles were ready for sharing a few things that they had made. Delia had knitted scarves for both May and Media and had made mittens for Charles and Willie.

"Oh Delia this is beautiful it's my favorite color," said May as she fingered the warm blue scarf.

"Well that would bring out your eyes," Delia remarked. "And Media your red scarf will compliment your dark eyes."

"Thank you mother," Media said giving her mother the present that she had made.

"What's this! Is this your work?" Exclaimed her mother.

Media told her how May had helped set out the words *Home Sweet Home* but she herself had done all the stitching plus the little picture of the house. Media was very proud of her work and she beamed as her mother told her that her work had improved.

"Here is my present mother," Charles said handing it to her. Delia opened the little package and inside was a wooden book holder.

"This will be so useful. You are so talented with your hands!" Charles showed her how he had carved the design on the end. "Well I am pleased," she smiled.

"Open your present Aunt Delia," urged May. She watched as Delia carefully pulled the tissue apart. May had embroidered a lovely handkerchief.

"Why May, when did you have time to do this? How sweet, I just love it! Thank you." Delia looked up and saw Mays appreciative eyes.

"Well Aunt Delia I have loved staying here with you and I wish I could do more," She beamed.

There was a knock on the door and immediately May knew it was Ed. Lyman. "I'll get it Aunt Delia," May rushed to the door and sure enough it was he. "Oh it's so nice to see you back when did you get in?" May questioned him. "Did you get caught in the storm?"

"Hold on girl let me get my coat off and I'll tell you all about it." Ed proceeded to shake off the snow and take off his boots while May hovered around him helping him with his bundles. "Everything went like clockwork. I met Mr. Harrison and finished the business for the farm. Then I had the rest of the time for shopping." He let May lead him into the parlor.

"Merry Christmas everyone! Mrs. Olney, this is for you," handling her a box wrapped in white with a red ribbon.

"Thank you that's so nice of you to remember me." She quickly untied the ribbon and opened the box; it was the most beautiful porcelain teapot. "This is lovely, the handpainted detail is exquisite, I can't thank you enough!" Delia couldn't believe her eyes. Now she could serve tea in style.

Ed was glad he could surprise her, " Now I'll expect tea every time I come," he said.

"Yes you will, we can have a tea party," answered Delia.

Ed passed a rectangular present to Media and a smaller parcel to Charles, "go ahead open them" he urged.

Media ripped off the paper and gasped, "look a book! It's *Little Women* by Louisa May Alcott!"

Charles couldn't believe his eyes when he unwrapped a small knife. He carefully turned it around in his hands. It was the perfect size for whittling."How did you know that was just what I wanted?" Charles exclaimed.

Ed grinned at him, "By the way you handle that type in the news office, you have talent in those hands," he answered.

Ed had been saving the little package for May until the others had finished opening their presents. May sat quietly waiting her turn. Ed wasn't to be rushed."May I saved yours until the last because it is the best." He went to her side. "If you accept this, you will make me the happiest man in the world." He knelt down as she unwrapped the small box and watched her face as she opened the box. May gazed at the ring with a green stone.

"Oh, it is my birth stone, an emerald!" she exclaimed turning to Ed.

"May born in May, " he said. "Will you do the honor of marrying me?"

"Yes, I accept." She leaned into him and gave him a small kiss on the lips, she was aware that the others were watching. "Come to help me in the kitchen I made a special cake for you." May took his hand and led him out of the room. When they were out of sight she hugged him feeling his warmth and their kiss was sweet and long.

How May had looked forward to this day. She could see ahead loving him and having a family. Her heart sang. They were to visit his family at the farm after lunch and announce the news.

"It looks like chocolate, my favorite," Ed said loudly.

Delia scurried to the kitchen and congratulated them. "That was nice to share your proposal with us! Now there is no question about it, except when the wedding will be."

Ed looked at May. She had been thinking that the springtime would be a good time. "When the flowers come out in April, what do you think?" she asked him.

"That's soon enough," he replied looking longingly into her light eyes.

They hardly noticed what was for lunch. The chocolate cake was delicious and tasted even better with the tea Aunt Delia served from her new teapot. May and Ed thanked Delia and gave the family hugs as they left for the Lyman farm.

It was an overcast day but still the sun seemed to brighten the clouds. Ed enjoyed being with May again and they talked of farming and how they needed more rain in the spring for the crops. He had hoped she would be impressed by the farm especially since he was provided 80 acres by his father. During the war he had driven government wagons and sent his earnings home to his father. The 80 acres was in return for the payments.

"This is where I'd like to start farming on my own," he told May. "It is good soil here and close enough to town to build a house." She agreed that it was a good location.

"It's wonderful to smell the clean air. A farming life gives you a freedom to make your own decisions." She wanted to support his interest in farming and show she thought highly of his choices.

They finally arrived at the Lyman farm. They stopped at the farm house where Ed's father Jonathan and mother Sarah lived. Ed was excited for them to meet May. She slid down easily from the wagon in his arms and was happy to have him escort her to the house. They crossed the porch and Ed introduced her to his father who opened the door.

"This is May Genevieve Rhubottom the smartest and sweetest lady in the land," he boasted. May blushed and held out her hand to Ed's father.

"It's my pleasure to meet you Mr. Lyman," she offered.

"The greater pleasure is mine Miss May." He took her hand, "If I have permission to call you by your first name. Ed has described you to me and I've looked forward to meeting you. You are undoubtedly the apple of his eye."

John called to his wife, "Sarah, come and meet May."

May blushed again and turned to Ed. "You didn't tell me he is so complementary."

"Well I do think highly of you and yet you have good practical sense," Ed replied. Seeing his mother coming to the door, he presented May to her. "This is May, Mother," taking off May's coat and putting it next to his. May had worn her best black skirt with a little bustle, and her white blouse with the lace at the collar and sleeves.

"How nice to meet you May." Mrs. Lyman looked her over thinking she was small and dainty.

"It was very hospitable of you to invite me to Christmas dinner." May spoke up to Ed's mother. She was tall and buxom and seemed pleasant enough smelling like turkey.

"We have news! May and I will be married! You will have a daughter-in-law," smiled Ed Lyman.

"When will the happy day occur?" Mrs. Lyman turned to May for the answer.

"We are thinking in April, when the flowers bloom," smiled May.

"That's a fitting time of year, before the corn is planted," John Lyman thought out loud.

"Do come into the parlor and meet the others." Mrs. Lyman indicated the way.

The fireplace was ablaze and the Christmas tree was large taking up a corner of the room. It was decorated with popcorn chains and handmade decorations. The rest of the family were in the middle of a guessing game. They all looked up when their brother Ed entered with May on his arm.

"I want you all to meet my fiancé May," Ed started the introductions. "May, this is William who runs the farm with father and me, Louisa my sister and her husband Ross Ackerman, Julia sitting down with Stella, and Silvester by the fireplace." They all welcomed May and had her sit by Silvester, with Ed standing next to his youngest brother.

"This is a big family, it's wonderful to meet all of you," remarked May looking at their faces reflecting the firelight.

"And they're not all here, there's three others" chimed in Stella the youngest at seven years.

"You must enjoy playing games together, let's continue," said May as Ed and she joined in. Each one had a riddle, and if you guessed it, then it was your turn to ask a riddle. Mr. and Mrs. Lyman came and sat on the settee by the door. They were very happy watching their family and occasionally John would answer one of the riddles with a ridiculous idea making everyone laugh hilariously.

Finally Mrs. Lyman stood up and asked Julia and Stella to help with the dinner.

"Please let me help too," offered May.

With a nod of her head Mrs. Lyman consented. As they walked through the dining room to the kitchen, May noticed the long table and the formal lace curtains. She could imagine the large family sitting at the long table. The kitchen in the back of the house was sizable with a small table to the side. May stopped while she admired the view from the windows. The backyard was large with bushes around it.

"Are those lilac bushes Mrs. Lyman?" asked May.

"Yes they have beautiful purple blooms in the Spring."

"Well that would be perfect to get married here in the backyard with the lilacs blossoming," remarked May. "That is if you approved of using your yard. Aunt Delia's place is in town and not as lovely as this," hesitated May.

"As long as you arrange everything yourself, dear" replied Mrs. Lyman. May focused her attention on helping Julia who was mashing the potatoes and needed a bowl.

"Use that big one with the blue design," Julia directed.

"You must be a whiz in this kitchen," May commented.

"Actually I'm helping my sister Ellen and living with her and her husband in town. She just had a baby and needs some help," answered Julia while she scraped the last of the potatoes in the bowl and gave it to Stella to take to the table. "They went to her husband's family for Christmas." The rest of the vegetables were put into bowls and May helped set the table with Stella. Mrs. Lyman had finished making the gravy and asked Julia to get Silvester to carry the turkey in.

"Don't forget the condiments, Stella, and dig some pickles out of the crock," ordered Mrs. Lyman.

May followed Stella into the buttry and held the plate as Stella pulled the pickles from the brine with tongs. Then May cut them into smaller pieces.

"Where do you go to school?" May asked Stella. She hadn't seen her in town.

"There's a farm school a few miles down the road, it goes to sixth grade. Then I'll be going to the school in town." Stella wrinkled her nose. The vinegar in the pickles was strong.

The family gathered around the dining table with Mr. and Mrs. Lyman at each end. The others filled in leaving the youngest at the end with their mother. May was impressed with the amount of food. Farm families eat simply but well. They all bowed their heads as Mr. Lyman said grace to thank the Lord for their many blessings.

After dinner Ed surprised them with some chocolates he brought from Kansas City. They savored their choice and thought it was the finest dinner ever.

The women cleared the table and spent time washing and cleaning up. Louisa wasn't feeling too well and suspected she was in the baby way. The women shared their stories and May felt included in the family. After relaxing in the parlor with the men for a little while, Louisa and Ross said their good-byes and set off before dark.

Putting on their coats Ed decided to show May the barn and out buildings. The barking of the farm dog greeted them but was hushed as he wiggled his way to their legs. The collie had spotted them coming out of the door and needed to investigate the new person. Ed reached down and patted him ."This is Laddie our dog" he chuckled, "he's always around when you don't need him."

May stroked the soft brown and white fur. "He's a fine friendly dog, he can come along with us."

The barn housed the horses, the cellar some pigs, and the huge hay loft provided plenty to eat for the horses during the winter. There was a grainery, and a workshop to repair equipment. Then there was a storage barn with a smaller workshop.

"We could add on to the storage barn, and have our own place here," Ed began. "Or it might be easier to build a small house just by itself." He looked at May quizzically.

"Our own house would be nice," gulped May. Things were going faster than she could think.

"Dearest May, I hoped you would like it here and I want you to share my life, I can't imagine it without you. I love you so much." Ed gallantly picked up her small hand and caressed it. May was giddy with delight that Ed wanted her, she felt warm all over.

"I do love you too" she whispered. Was this what falling in love was? Looking up to his warm gaze, he tenderly kissed her small lips. May was engulfed in their own dream wishing it could go on uninterrupted. However it was getting late and they should start back.

Ed hitched up the horse and they thanked the family for a wonderful Christmas dinner. On the way back to Aunt Delia's the clouds had cleared and the moon shone on the dirt road. May looked at the stars overhead while Ed cradled her in the curve of his arm. His body swayed with the movement of his horse and wagon. May could hardly believe that she and Ed had agreed to get married. Was this what God wanted for them? It seemed right and natural. She checked Ed's smiling face and she smiled back relaxing in his arms feeling comfortable and happy. Arriving back in town, Ed helped May out and walked her to the porch.

"Do you want to come in?" May asked.

"It's been a long day for you, as much as I'd like to. You need to get your rest. I'll see you in church tomorrow." Ed gave a kiss on her cold nose and then a lingering kiss on her quivering lips. "I'll be thinking of you all night, sweet May."

It was all May could do to stumble in through the door. "I'll be dreaming of you too, dear Ed," she managed to say. Later May confided to Aunt Delia about her feelings for Ed. "I do love him" she sighed.

"Well it's about time you realize that he's the one for you," Delia retorted. "you've been in the clouds for months now, it's high time you know what a good man he is and how you both can start building a life together."

1870
MAY'S WEDDING

The time went by before the wedding while May was busy sewing her wedding dress.. It had long sleeves, a fitted bodice, ruffles down the front to the floor, and a small bustle. Her room was covered in pieces of creamy fabric. May wrote to Mother Painter about all the plans, knowing she wouldn't be able to come with her newborn child Cora, born January 17. May was content that Alice was going to be her maid-of-honor, Media and Julia her bridesmaids, and Stella the flower-girl. Cousin Katie hoped to come with Alice and bring Mattie, her oldest daughter of four. Mr. Kent would take care of Fannie for a couple of days. The wedding was scheduled for the first Saturday in May when the lilacs would be in full bloom.

May was in her dream and finished the last term of teaching in a blur. Helping Aunt Delia at the newspaper office was coming to a close. Delia had someone interested in buying the *Plaindealer* and she would be able to retire. and finish bringing up little Willie and see Media through school.

Meanwhile Ed was building a small house with the help of William and Silvester. It had a good size kitchen with room for a table, a parlor, and a bedroom. They could always add on if need be. As the days grew longer Ed had May come to see how the progress was going. She was glad that he built a bed, and that Mr. and Mrs. Lyman gave them a small table and two chairs. Finally it was time for May to move her belongings and set up the house.

The weekend approached and May started to get the food ready. She spent the time in Mrs. Lyman's kitchen preparing a fruit cake to pass out as the dream cake. She baked bread and churned butter for the sandwiches. Lastly she cooked chicken and baked a gold layer cake spread with butter icing.

When Ed took her back to Delia's, May was looking forward to seeing Alice and Katie who would be staying in her room. This was the last night that May would be Delia's family guest. They arrived the next day with Mattie and freshened up with some lunch.

It was time to go to the Lyman farm and Ed had a team of horses this time, and set up more seats to accommodate the extra company and Delia's family. The sun had warmed the air into a comfortable outdoor wedding day atmosphere. May was chatting with Alice and Katie while Mattie was lulled to sleep during the ride. Ed stopped the horses in the Lyman farm drive and helped everyone down from the wagon. The women went to help May get ready and Ed unhitched the horses. He had to change too.

The pastor pranced in on his horse and was ushered to the back yard. All of Ed's brothers and sisters were there except Charles who was still in the army.

Mrs Lyman had offered the downstairs bedroom for May and the bridesmaids to change into their dresses. Alice had a lavender gown fitted in the front and the skirt pulled back into a bustle. A long sleeved jacket and brimmed hat completed her outfit. Media and Julia had long fuller skirts of lavender with sewn pleated rows around the bottom. Their blouses had matching lavender sleeves with a ruffled white insert in the front. They had made circlets of violets for their hair. Stella at seven years looked sweet in a white dotted Swiss dress with a lavender sash tied in a bow at the back. Media had made a violet circlet for her hair too. She handed Stella a small basket of apple blossom petals to sprinkle on the grass. Media had also picked a hand bouquet of lilies-of-the-valley for May. The sweet smell made everyone sigh. Delia swished them out to the backyard and gave May a hug. She was wearing her Sunday black skirt and jacket with a brooch and a brimmed hat.

"You are the sweetest bride, May born in May. I wish all the joys of married life out-weigh the disappointments that happen down the path."

May beamed back, "Thank you for all you've done for me Aunt Delia." She adjusted the lovely veil that Aunt Orphy and Uncle Lawrence had sent her.. They stepped out to the sunny yard filled with lilacs and smiling faces of the family. The men looked especially handsome in their Sunday suits. May walked toward Ed steadied by Delia's arm. She was mesmerized by his blue eyes.

Ed was thinking he had the loveliest bride. Her veil didn't hide her fair skin delicately framed by her brown hair pulled up in a bun with ringlets at the sides of her face. Her light blue green eyes found his as Delia gave her away putting their hands together. They were transfixed as they repeated the vows after the minister. Alice held May's bouquet while Ed slid the gold band on May's slender finger. The moment came when Ed lifted her veil and softly covered her lips with his.

The minister announced, "This is Mr. and Mrs. Edmund Lyman." Everyone clapped.

Alice was the first to hug May. "You look so beautiful, dear sister May. This is a day you'll never forget,"

"Oh Alice, you'll find someone too!" May thanked her.

John and Sarah welcomed her into the family. "We are so pleased to have you in our family as Ed's wife," Sarah gave May a quick squeeze. "I know you'll make Ed happy."

"You make us all happy," John put a big kiss on her cheek. "Congratulations Ed, you picked a sweet peach for a wife." He winked at May and made her blush.

"I'm a happy man," Ed agreed.

William was impatient to kiss the bride, a peck on the cheek. May was grateful for all his help building the house with Ed. She pulled him back and gave him a kiss on the cheek. This time William blushed; he didn't want to get in trouble with his brother.

"It's alright today," Ed slapped William on the arm. "You need to get your own girl."

Louisa and Ross congratulated Ed. Louisa looked stunning in a blue dress and hat. "May this is a lovely wedding! I understand you made your gown? You are a very good seamstress." cooed Louisa.

"You look radiant May. The choice of lavender for the dresses was lovely next to the lilacs, how did you pick the perfect day?" Ellen chimed in holding her sleeping baby.

"God blessed us today!" smiled May.

Mattie Kent came running through the gathering chased by Willie. "You pulled my hair," she complained.

"Well you flung it in my face," retorted Willie.

"Now children," chided Katie trying to reason with two four year olds.

After everyone greeted the bride and groom, they made their way slowly to the house. Mother Lyman had set up a buffet table in the dining room with the chicken sandwiches, tea, and layered cake.

There was a separate plate with the individual wrapped pieces of fruit cake to take home and put under their pillow to dream on. The women would certainly do that, especially the unmarried ones.

John and Sarah beckoned to May and Ed to proceed to the parlor and open the stack of wedding presents. Ed helped May open the gifts of dishes, pots and pans, kitchen utensils, bedding, hand-embroidered pillowcases, a quilt from Delia, crocheted doilies, and many other hand made items.

May was overwhelmed with everything. After thanking the family and friends May touched Ed's arm. "Ed, please take me outside for some air," she whispered.

He immediately obliged. The cool air soothed May; and the lilacs nodded in the lengthening shadows. She felt the soft grass under her thin slippers, and Ed's strong arm around her waist.

"This is a wonderful day Ed Lyman," she purred.

"You are a wonderful woman May Lyman," he replied pleased to use her new name. They kissed to the beginning of their new life together. Arm in arm they returned to their wedding celebration. Many family stories were told and laughter filled the house.

When it was time for the guests to return home, May climbed the stairs and threw her bouquet to the three unmarried girls aiming for Alice, who jumped to catch it.

"I'm next," Alice called out.

William drove Delia's group back to town giving Ed a chance to scoop up May in his arms and carry her into their new home.

1871
MAY'S BABY FREDDIE

Now that May and Ed were married, May was happy to settle into keeping house and cooking for Ed. Their idea of a honeymoon was sharing lemonade in the afternoon and making love on their new bed. May welcomed every advance and soon the morning sickness was her next adventure. Starting a family right away was what they wanted. The hot months of the summer didn't make it any easier and by fall May felt much better and harvested the root vegetables and squash from the garden. They had eaten well from the garden, but the corn crop wasn't as good as what Ed expected. It was hard to cultivate corn with only one horse. He planned to plant more corn for next year's crop.

The early winter was uneventful. May sewed some baby clothes and Ed made a cradle. Christmastime was spent with the Lyman family. Ellen brought her baby to visit and everyone was fawning over her. Louisa and Ross didn't come to the Lyman farm since they had their baby in August and lived so far away. May received a lovely white blanket from mother and father Lyman, and a sleeping bunting and a knitted sweater and cap also. Some soft flannel fabric was sent by Delia which May hemmed into several receiving blankets to wrap the baby in. Media had sent some washcloths and a towel. May stuffed a pillow case with cotton batting for a cradle mattress.

It was good that Ed kept Delia informed about May's progress. By the end of January May felt it would be soon. Ed was ready to get the doctor and pick up Delia whenever May said it was time. The pains started to come on the eve of February 2nd and by morning a fine baby boy arrived. Delia had stayed all night along with the doctor. After breakfast the doctor left and Delia gave May some instruction on nursing the baby. Ed watched over them as they slept most of the day with several feedings for the baby.

May was determined to be the best mother she could be. Ed was happy to have a son. They named him Johnathan Fredrick for both Ed's father and May's grandfather John.. Fredrick was their favorite name so they called him Freddie.

The rest of the winter was taken with the care of Freddie. Ed would come in from work to find May making supper while Freddie finished his nap. Ed held him during his fussy time as May cleaned up and did some baking.

"I hope the corn will be a good price this year," Ed thought out loud. "And you little Freddie can help me pick it," he looked into the tiny face. Freddie was transfixed on his father's face and didn't make a peep.

May was thinking of planting the spring garden. The weather was far from warm; next month April would be the right time. She had kept some bean seeds and squash seeds for planting.

"Do you have enough corn seed this year Mr. Lyman?" she asked Ed.

"No, I'll have to pick up some more to cover the rest of the acreage." He mumbled something about the corn costs and transferred Freddie to May's lap for his final feeding. May hummed and nursed their baby then settled him in the cradle and tucked him in. She waited for the bread to finish baking and retired for the night. Ed followed shortly after. They both would be awakened quite early by the baby.

Spring was very busy, Alice came to see the baby and visit with May. The two of them fussed over Freddie and watched him try to turn over. They went for walks and the fresh air made Freddie sleep better. Alice hadn't any luck yet finding a serious admirer.

She was still living with Katie and helping her with the girls. Alice was restless and thought she might visit mother Painter and see her dear brothers and sisters again. She rattled on about plans and hoped May could go too, but May was content to stay put for the time being.

By mid summer, Ed was assessing his investment in the corn crop. Even though he had planted his 80 acres with corn, he still couldn't cover his costs at 15 cents a bushel. He was very upset and went to talk with his father. The door banged behind him as he entered the farmhouse.

"I'm ready to sell out and do something else!" he announced loudly to John.

"Calm down Ed , there's lots of other things to do." John motioned him to sit down. "I've heard that Horace Greeley is setting up a colony in Colorado," he started. "I knew him in his younger days and he seemed to get things going in the right direction. Maybe you could look him up and see what's going on out there," John planted the idea in Ed's head.

"Colorado is a beautiful location." Ed remembered when he was there during the war driving government wagons by the Platte River. The soil was rich in the grasslands and would be better for crops. Ed slapped his knee, "By golly! That's a great idea. I can't wait to tell May," Out the door with a bang and off to his own little house.

May had supper on the table and Freddie had been fed. He gurgled happily on the floor trying to grab his stuffed bunny. Ed washed up and sat down with a glint in his eye. He thanked the Lord for their food and for their many blessings. May sensed something was up but didn't dare ask since corn prices were so bad.

"How would you like to go to Colorado and live," Ed dove right in. He was concerned how May would feel about such a move.

May gasped, she certainly hadn't expected this. She smoothed her apron on her lap and biting her lip managed to say, "I've read that it's very beautiful there."

"We'd sell this place and buy a covered wagon and team of horses so you and Freddie could ride and take our things." Ed continued hoping May would like the idea.

"It sounds possible," she hesitated. " When were you thinking of doing this?" May asked, getting more interested in his plans. She passed him some more potatoes and carrots.

"If I could sell as soon as possible before the winter, then we could leave right away while it's still good weather. I remember the route I took along the Little Blue River to Grand Island on the Platte, then to Cottonwood Springs and then along the South Platte River," He went on.

"It must be a long trip. Do we have to worry about Indians?" May inquired.

"Since there have been many wagon trains going through this route to make claims, and it's a government trail, I don't think we'd see much of the Indians," he answered.

It was in the past ten years that hundreds of thousands of wagons traveled along the Platte River. Sations had built up along the way about every twelve miles to giving rest stops to the wagoners . It was common for settlers to see 1500 wagons pass a day. Freight wagons were going both east and west with supplies and new pioneers were on the way west. Then the trail forked, one along the North Platte River to Idaho, the other by the South Platte River to Colorado. Indian attacks had increased during 1868 and some people were killed and scalped. This led to the Indian wars. The headquarters for the soldiers was Fort McPherson at Cottonwood Springs.

Ed explained to May, "Most of the fighting was south of Fort McPherson when the Pawnee were under the command of Major

North besides the regular cavalry. By using the Indians it helped to understand the Sioux warfare. The Pawnee hated the Sioux and were very motivated in fighting them. There was also a band of scouts under Buffalo Bill Cody. The battles started when General Carr came up from the Republican River with several companies of U.S. Troops following the Sioux on the move to the Platte.

The Sioux were caught in the sand hills and scattered only to be sandwiched by Buffalo Bill and the companies of soldiers which had separated on different trails." Ed recalled that he was glad to be out of there by then.

"Some 600 Sioux warriors were discovered on the third day by Buffalo Bill, and the companies which had joined each other had hid in the ravines near the Platte. Thanks to Buffalo Bill the Sioux Chief Tall Bull was killed. General Carr fought the battle at Summit Springs in July of 1869 killing the Sioux warriors and loosing many soldiers and Pawnees. This battle brought an end to the Indian wars." Ed could see May was riveted to the seat.

"It's a shame to think of all that killing," she sighed. "Didn't the Indians attack the railroad as well?" May questioned.

"That was the end of the attacks on the railroad in Nebraska," Ed replied. He got up and cleared the table.

"The railroad brought cattle out for the herders to start raising cattle. There must be lots of ranches built up," envisioned May. She could picture a peaceful journey along a well populated route.

"There still could be stealing of cattle and horses from the ranches," Ed added. I even heard that Buffalo Bill's horse was stolen this spring and so far he hasn't managed to get it back. He'll have to stick to hunting buffalo," he chuckled.

"Well, if the Lord is willing, I'll be ready to go to Colorado," May finally answered Ed's first question. She proceeded to get Freddie ready for bed.

WAGON TRIP

Ed was eager to start the plan to go to Colorado. It didn't take him long to find a buyer; everyone did farming and his 80 acres was close to town. He sold it for $800. and bought a team of horses and a new covered wagon. May was amazed at how fast everything was happening. She had no trouble packing the few things they had, pots and pans, bedding and clothes. Her books fit into the trunk with pictures of her family. Ed took apart the bed and strapped it on the side of the wagon. Some barrels held the root vegetables. They would fish and hunt for meat.

They said goodbye to the Lymans. Sarah and John waved from the porch. Ed was pleased that his father suggested Colorado. He felt it was the right move. They stopped in Garnett to see Delia.

"Aunt Delia it's going to be an adventure!" May gave her a big hug."You'll have to come and visit us when we get settled," she said giving Media and the two brothers a squeeze.

"This is the time for you two and little Freddie to do whatever comes along," advised Delia.

Ed gave her a hug. "Thank you for all you've done for us."

"We'll miss you," May started tearing up.

"Now may the Lord watch over you and keep you safe," Aunt Delia comforted her.

Ed helped May back up on the wagon. Delia gave Freddie a kiss and handed him to Ed who reached up and plopped him in May's arms.

They were off through the farmlands of Kansas heading north to the Little Blue River. They passed small towns and would occasionally stop for supplies. Little Freddie would sit on May's lap or nap in the wagon. She had cushions to sit on to keep from getting sore. It was a warm September and still a little dry. The dust was kicked up by the horses so they wore handkerchiefs around their faces. It took them only a few days to get to Blue Rapids where the Little Blue and Big Blue forked. And another four days to the Platte River.

May was excited to see the big river. She loved the water and would take a dip while she did the washing. The nights were cool and gave them a welcome relief from the sunny days. Camping by the river the foliage was green with more humidity. They listened to the insects singing and gazed at the stars in the clear skies. Sleep came easy after bouncing around all day. Freddie got them up early with his hungry cry.

One evening while May was swimming in the river they were surprised by another party appearing with their team and wagon.

"Ed, someone's coming," May scurried into the wagon to put on her clothes. Ed had been playing with Freddie and immediately picked him up and watched as the wagon came to a stop.

A father and two sons jumped down and called out, "This looks like a good spot." They unhitched the horses and took care of them.

"Hey Maw, you'll like it here," one of the son's yelled.

"It's always full of bugs, I've got so many bites." Maw appeared with another woman and young girl. She swatted and complained as they descended from the wagon.

Ed asked, "Where are you from?"

"Arkansas," the father answered. "We're going to Puget Sound or bust."

"Mostly bust," added one of the sons.

"We are on the way to Colorado," Ed stated.

The young girl rushed past them on the way to the river.

"Now don't you go into the river and get your clothes all wet," yelled her mother. "I don't want to have to wash your clothes on

In the vast semi-arid areas of the Oregon trail, animals had to eat at least ten-to-twelve hours at night for enough strength to pull the wagons and produce milk. The quality of the grasses was the main reason oxen were used instead of horses. oxen can work on a poorer nutritional diet than horses. there are many journal accounts of a late start in the morning because the belled oxen could not be found. Wagon train of one hundred wagons would have at least four-to-six hundred oxen or more, milk cows, draft horses, and saddle horses. a hundred wagons could not make a circle the grass inside any circle would be tramped down and covered with several inches of manure in a matter of hours. Picture and Text From Historical Facts of the Oregon Trail and Western Expansion by O. Ned Eddins, www.thefurtrapper.com/oregon trail.htm.

top of everything else." She shook her head and went about getting the food ready to cook.

The men looked around for firewood. It was picked over, already fairly bare from others stopping there.

"Here you can share our fire," Ed invited them. We'll be turning in early.

Maw came over and spoke to May. "Well what do we have here? What a cute baby. What's his name?" Maw chucked him under his chin.

"Freddie, he's almost eight months old." May placed him on the ground. He sat there holding on to May's skirt and looked up at the strange woman.

"He's got blue eyes the color of the sky, I don't know how you can travel with a baby, they're so fussy. I have enough trouble with my sister's girl." complained Maw.

"Freddie's very good. He cut some teeth before we left and doesn't cry very much now." May tried to be positive. She started to feed him some mushed oats.

Maw returned to the campfire and proceeded to order the sons around. They were quite loud quarreling over the food.

When May was trying to get Freddie asleep in the wagon, their loud voices were very aggravating. They stayed up late drinking and laughing. It was hard for May to sleep too. Ed was keeping an eye on the fire until it burned out.

At first Ed was glad to have other people to travel with. Especially since he was anxious about Indians. But after several nights of their loud neighbors, Ed decided to shake them and camp at the next farm instead. Ed and the little family headed off early continuing along the wide trail left by the wagon trains. He tried to keep the wagon away from the rutted road. The Platte meandered along the plains. The sky's reflection in the water was a contrasting blue against the warm hues of the grasslands making a winding trail as far as the eye could see. May was content to let the scenery go by and little Freddie was lulled to sleep by the gentle lurching of the wagon.

The days blended together and the nights became colder. They kept warm under the quilts in the wagon. Each evening gave them some exercise time. May did the washing in the river and the baths were cold as the water had become colder. It was a welcome relief to stop at a farmhouse and ask to stay close by. The families were always friendly and shared some baked goodies with them.

One late afternoon when they stopped at a ranch a bearded rough looking fellow came over to the wagon and called to Ed. who immediately started slapping him on the back as a long lost buddy.

"Where have you been all these years, Duffy," Ed began.

"Jist hangen around these here parts mostly at Fort McPherson, me boy." He pulled on his beard and took off his tattered hat.

"Looks like you went and got yerself a missus, and a youngen too," Duffy observed. "Howdy Ma'am, nice to meetcha. This here's my buddy from the mule whacken days in the gov'nment. He was jist a whippersnapper back then." He bowed his head a couple of times.

Ed introduced his sweetie May and little Freddie. "Duffy saved my skin on the trail," he explained to May. "He kept the bunch of us cheered up with his stories."

"Any friend of my husband is welcome in our family," May greeted him in spite of his ugly looks.

"Any God fearing bloke is honored by your company ma'am," Duffy returned. He shifted his attention to Ed. "Now Ed, how's 'at you're travelen this di-rection?" His raspy voice was hard to understand.

"We're figuring on starting up a farm in Colorado and making a better go at it than in Kansas." Ed looked at him.

"There's no prettier spot than in Colorado." Duffy stared at the horizon as if he could see the mountains looming up. "I woun't travel alone though. A small In'jin party can take one wagon, but mostly their after horses. There's a group of wagons jist ahead of you that you'd cetch up to.

Ed alerted by his friend's warning planned to take off early in the morning. He spent the rest of the evening swapping stories with Duffy. May went to sleep by the exchange of voices she heard from the campfire.

The next morning Ed and May broke camp before sunrise. The clouds were pink and soon the sun's rays warmed the couple as they sat on the buckboard. Freddie had been fed and was reaching for anything he could grasp. May tried to keep him busy with some spools strung on a string. The day wore on and May settled Freddie back for a nap and joined him. Meanwhile Ed had spied a couple of horseback riders coming across the plains. Getting closer he could make out that they were soldiers by their looks. Ed stowed his gun back under the seat. Riding up to the wagon the men signaled Ed to stop.

"Just want to make sure everything is all right with you," one soldier called out.

"Haven't had any sign of Indians," Ed replied. "If that's what you mean."

"We're trying to keep an eye on the wagon trail so folks are safe," he answered. "There's some wagons ahead of you. You'll see them by tomorrow." He touched his hat in a mock salute.

"Thanks, I'm trying to catch up with them instead of traveling alone." Ed saluted back.

They headed off in the direction the wagon came from and soon disappeared on the horizon.

"What was that all about?" asked May sticking her head out of the wagon.

"Looks as if we have a government patrol on duty," Ed smiled at May. "We'll catch up to the others tomorrow."

May sleepily grinned and poked her head back in. She hoped they would be safe and said a prayer for their safe journey. That night after tending the horses, Ed didn't build a campfire. They were up at the crack of dawn to get a head start. Sure enough by mid-day they could see the dust from the wagons in the distance and by late afternoon they caught up with them. They didn't seem to mind another wagon. When they stopped for the night Ed visited their campfire to let them know who they were. May was still tired and didn't have much patience with Freddie who wanted to crawl around on the ground. He needed a bath but May wiped him with a cloth. Everything was covered in dust. and May could hardly wait to get to Cottonwood Springs to do some cleaning.

Luckily the other wagons were going to spend a day in town when they reached it the next night. They needed supplies and it gave the horses a well earned rest. May shook out the bedding and heated some water for a sponge bath. Freddie had a splashing time and even Ed laughed at his antics.

"There seems to be a lot of people in town" commented Ed. "It's certainly grown since I saw the town last. I picked up a newspaper at the store, let see what it has to say about the area."

May went about packing the supplies in the wagon while Freddie investigated around the wagon.

"Says here that the Railroad line from Michigan to the North Platte is completed and many families have come by train under the planning of Mr. Lee to the North Platte to find homes," Ed read. "I would think they would rather live here or someplace else then the North Platte. As I recall that's a very rough place to raise a family." Ed kept an eye on Freddie who was crawling towards one of the wagon wheels.

"I'm glad we're not going to the North Platte," said May. "The fork in the river is fairly close where we go south on the Platte, isn't that right?" she questioned him.

"Yes this is the turning point, from now on it will be all gradually uphill on the South Platte," he answered.

"Have you met any of the wagon families?" asked May.

"I saw a family with some younger children. Then there's one where the son was bad mouthing his mother. Looks like the wagons are starting to congregate here at the edge of town, you can see for yourself," Ed pointed.

May looked up at the wagons parading toward them. The first one had a young couple sitting on the buckboard. The second had an old man and two women aboard, with a young man walking alongside. Next was a couple with a girl and boy. Then came the young family with at least four children, one a baby. The last one was the older couple and an older boy.

"I'm going to meet the children," May said to Ed. She picked up Freddie and went to where the wagons were setting up for the night.

Ed busied himself with the horses and packed the feed. He was glad to be traveling with the other wagons. There wasn't any more talk of Indians, but Duffy was wise to advise them.

After breakfast the next morning when all the wagons were ready, they rolled out of town. The way was very rutted and May couldn't seem to get Freddy comfortable. In the afternoon they picked up the South Platte river and watched the North Platte River coming from Idaho flow past the town of the same name. The South Platte was not as wide now and the grasslands stretched out as far as the eye could see.

When they stopped to make camp, Ed unhitched the horses and went to pick up buffalo dung to make a fire. May fed Freddie and boiled a supper of potatoes, carrots, and dried beef. That night the stars seemed to be brighter than ever. The other families were going through the bedtime routine punctuated by the loudmouthed son berating his mother. Ed was appalled that he was within hearing distance.

"Hasn't he learned a bit of decency!" Ed exclaimed. He could stand it no longer and made his way to him. Pulling him aside Ed started to reprimand him. "How dare you use language like that to your mother. She gave you life and raised you for the love of God! It doesn't make you a man to cuss. A man is known for respect he shows to others, especially his mother!" Edmund was squeezing his upper arm like a vice, and the boy was red faced and embarrassed.

"You can't tell me not to cuss," the boy blurted.

"I just did. Not only is it disrespectful, but it shows you have not grown up yet. Think about it. Think about what you say!" Ed left the boy standing there gawking at him.

"I'm not going to stand for any more of his badmouthing," Ed stated to May as he removed his boots and climbed into the wagon.

The next few days Ed's wagon pulled ahead of the other wagons. They had passed Julesburg which meant they had made it to Colorado. The sky was so blue reflecting in the river. May stared at the clouds hanging on the horizon.

"Oh look," she pointed at the clouds, "the mountains must be under the clouds." Sure enough one lone peak showed under the clouds. Only Longs Peak was tall enough to be seen. Later when they got to Ft. Morgan it was too dark to see anymore.

"It won't be long now!" Ed told May in excitement, "you'll see how pretty Colorado is!"

May had already fallen in love with the grasslands. There were some late blossoming flowers amidst the tall grass, although most of the grasses had turned mustard and ochre color. The wagon trail was still trodden down into a dusty crust. They were lucky that it hadn't rained and turned the ground to mud.

On their last leg of the journey, the mountains joined together forming a long line against the horizon. They appeared blue being so far away yet seeming to be closer. Finally they could see the town of Greeley, the clouds were covering the sky thick with moisture and a light rain accompanied them into town.

1872
COLORADO COLONY

Ed secured a room at the rooming house and the little family settled in trying to figure out what to do next. He found out there was no more desirable land left in the Greeley Colony, but there was a company in Longmont called the Chicago-Colorado Colony that seemed very promising.

Since the Greeley Union Colony had been such a success the year before, many colonies were starting up to attract the pioneers. The Greeley Colony was set up as a cooperation for investors to make money selling land to the pioneers who wanted to come west and farm and live in a beautiful healthful area. Descriptions of the mountains teeming with wildlife, plains ready to be planted, and rivers for water were included in the newspapers along with the investment property to entice the eastern people to come and live the dream of a lifetime. Everyone was reading about the possibilities of life in Colorado.

The Chicago-Colorado Colony was set up similarly to the Greeley Colony. It had started in earnest in 1871 to attract the hard workers of all trades and skills The membership fee of $155 ($5 being the initiation fee) included voting rights. It promised 5 to 40 acres of land depending on the distance from town, and the privilege of buying one business and one residential lot in town at $20 to $50 each. Each lot had to be improved by one year's time in order to obtain the title.

Seth Terry, the Colony President, purchased 60,000 acres east of Longs Peak near the St. Vrain River and the Big Thompson River. The area for the town had been chosen for its higher elevation with the St. Vrain Creek to the south and Little Thompson River to the north. (Based on some local folklore about flooding in the area) Unlike most colonies which were centered around the railroads, the town was six miles from the nearest railroad, a newly completed line from the Erie coal fields to Denver. (In May 1873, two years after the first settlers arrived in Longmont, the first train arrived from Golden, CO.)

Mr. Terry, after helping the colony write their constitution and by-laws, left his wife and eleven children in Chicago for five months to set up a place for people to sleep and eat in Longmont while the families could complete building their homes. By the end of the summer of 1871 there were 250 people working on the town. Ditches for water were built. The wells that were dug did not provide water that was fit to drink. Water barrels were set up behind the cabins and were filled by a water wagon owned by an enterprising Burlington resident. Saplings were planted to eventually give shade.

Because of the slight slope the town was on and its ever looming presence of Longs Peak, it was named 'Longmont'. The colony actually moved some of the buildings from the neighboring town of Burlington to Longmont. Half of the population, about 75 people, joined the colony. This made a bigger community which promised industry, temperance, and morality. The colony warned that anyone caught drinking in Longmont would lose their voting and land rights. One of the buildings that was moved from Burlington was a saloon which mysteriously burned down a week later.

Mr. Lyman went to Longmont twenty miles south of Greeley to secure a title for $150 for 40 acres of land that was three miles south of Longmont and a lot in town to build a cabin.

When the Lymans arrived in Longmont Main Street had a hotel, grocery & drug store, the Colony Office, furniture store, dry goods store, a bank, a library, and a church. There was a lumberyard, wagon depots, blacksmiths, butcher, barber, lawyer, physicians, insurance agent, bakery, dressmaker, livery stable, miller, and carpenters.

Mr. Lyman having bought in the Colony was busy putting up a small cabin for May and Freddie. They stayed at the rooms that welcomed the pioneers until their homes were ready. It didn't take long for their living quarters to be done and May gratefully moved their things in. Now May had more room to cook and care for her husband and son.

Ed had found a printing office just starting up in Longmont and he helped set it up and get the paper out during the winter months. Ed was doing his best to get the land ready for crops. Even though it had been surveyed for irrigation, the ditches took a while to put in. In the spring of 1872 Ed had five acres under irrigation.

"May it would be better to live on our land to raise crops," Ed surprised her as he entered the cabin with muddy boots. He quickly removed them and went to the wash bowl to clean his face and hands.

"How will we live there without a house?" May asked raising her eyebrows.

"We'll move the house out on two wagons," he answered picking up Freddie who was toddling toward him. "How's my big helper?

Longmont's Farmers Mill with wagon loads of bagged flour ready to be delivered. The sign above the door proclaims Longmont Farmers Mill ~ Pride of the Rockies, "Colorado's Famous Flour".

Submitted by Katharine Oliver

The Emerson and Buckingham Bank, Longmont's first bank, was established in 1871.

Submitted by the Longmont Daily Times-Call

Longmont, as it appeared in 1872, the first year of the town's existence. The St. Vrain Hotel and Colony buildings are shown in the 300 block on the east side of Main Street.

Submitted by the Longmont Daily Times-Call

Views and Visions from *A history of Longmont, Longmont Daily Times Call*

Are you helping your mother?" he quizzed him looking into his blue eyes. Freddie nodded and wiggled to be let down to the freedom of the floor.

May laughed, "I can see the house balanced on two wagons, you must be joking?"

"No joke dear, plenty of others have had success with it and the distance is only three miles. It should work fine as long as the weather is clear." Ed filled the bowls with the stew on the stove and May washed Freddie's hands. They sat down for supper thanking God for the food.

"It will be good to have a garden again," May thought out loud.

"I will be fencing the land," Ed added. With his team he was equipped for hauling logs and also for cultivating the crops.

MAY'S LETTER TO FRANK, MARCH 11, 1872

Longmont, Colo. March 11, 1872

Dear Brother Frank;

I suppose you wonder why I have not written sooner in reply to the letter you sent several weeks ago. The only reason is because there was nothing of any consequence to write. It has been a long cold and dull winter-so much so that times are very hard and business dull. But spring has come at last and things begin to look brighter. Most of the colonists come here expecting that Colorado never had cold weather and so many of them have seen pretty hard times. As for us, we have managed to get along without getting into debt and that is about all. It cost a great deal to buy everything for a team and family. But we are not discouraged in the least for we could not have done better in any new place the first year. Every day that I spend in Colorado makes me love it more and I do not think I could be induced to leave here now. How I wish you could stand by my side now and enjoy the scenery as I do. It was cloudy this morning but now the sky is clear and the sun shines warm and bright. The mountains look very clear and distinct and seem to be not more than two or three miles from here although it is nine miles to the foot hills. Long's peak rises clear above all the rest, stretching his white capped head 15000 feet in the air. Along the range both north and south rise great white peaks glittering in the sunshine like polished marble. We can see Pike's Peak away in the south so that we have over 150 miles of the Rocky Mountains in plain sight. The plains are looking better now for they are already beginning to look green and in all directions. I see farmers busy plowing or fencing. Mr. Lyman has gone to the St. Urain canyon today for fence posts and will be gone all night. If a man has a team his fence will cost next to nothing but his time and labor as the immense pine forests in the mountains are all free to all. We have sold our lot in town and will move out on our farm next week. We have bought 40 acres but that is all a man needs in Colorado for they can harvest as much from one acre here as they do from three in most of the states. I am anxious to get on our farm for it is nearly time to put in a garden. I have not heard from Rensselaer in a long time. But as you wrote he was on his way out here I shall not be surprised to see him any day. I hope he will come soon for it is a long time since I have seen him. How strange it will seem it will seem to sit in our little home at the foot of the Rocky mountains and talk over old times. Freddie's big blue eyes are closed in sleep just now or I could not write very well. He walks alone and is trying to talk some. He is a dear little pet and has been my comfort this winter for I have been obliged *to stay alone so much of the time. I think he looks very much as you did at his age. I cannot imagine how you look now and wish I had your picture. I suppose you and Willie will be very busy this spring. Give my love to Cora and Willie. I would like to see them very much. Tell Ma I will write to her before long and send my love to her in this. I also send respects to Mr. Painter and all who chance to inquire for me. Please write soon and often to your loving sister.*

May G. Lyman Box 86.

ALICE MEETS ISAAC

May was astounded when she received a letter from Alice about coming to Longmont. The Kansas – Denver RR was completed and a section north to Longmont. With the arrival of Alice on the train, May was so happy to have her sister there to help move and share this exciting time together. However, Alice happened to meet an eligible bachelor who was in the same mind of getting married.

When they met at the hardware store in Longmont, Alice was immediately fascinated by his looks. He was tall and lean from hard work and sported a beard that was neatly trimmed.

She whispered to May, "Do you know that man? Can you introduce me?"

May was taken aback, she knew him because Ed would go to cut posts at the Lower St. Vrain and would stay overnight with him.

"Alice I would like you to meet Isaac Richardson, he lives on a ranch at the Lower St. Vrain." May introduced them. "And this is my sister, Alice, fresh from Kansas."

"Good afternoon May and Alice," Isaac addressed them and shook Alice's hand. "I'm pleased to meet you Alice, are you staying long?" he looked at her dark hair and petite form. Her eyes were intently watching him.

"I'll be staying as long as I'm welcome. May can always use some help," answered Alice lowering her eyes.

"Well I hope she doesn't keep you too busy, for I would like to call on you sometime," he waited for his intent to sink in.

"Thank you, that would be quite possible," Alice looked at him with a smile.

"I will be helping Ed to move his house so I will be around," Isaac tipped his hat and left the women standing in the store.

He found many excuses to visit the Lymans and was smitten by Alice. They tied the knot with a Justice of the Peace before the month was over. May and Ed stood up for them and Alice and Isaac

The first street built in the town of Longmont. This was the west side of the street facing south 1872. Picture from Longmont Public Library, Copyright 2010 by Richard M. Hachett, *Longmont Times Call*

were in their own world of love. Since Isaac's ranch was 20 miles from Longmont, May only saw Alice when she came into town.

HOUSE MOVING

Moving the house proved to be the feat that was the talk of the town. Ed had rented a couple of freight wagons and four teams of oxen. A few workers from the freight company helped jack up the house and position the blocks to get the wagons underneath. As they slowly traveled along the road the men walked the three miles along the sides to make sure the house did not tip.

May watched them start off and was grateful that it was a small house. All the neighbors came along to see how it worked out. What a sight to see a cabin traveling down the road pulled by oxen. By the end of the day, and much heavy work, the house was positioned on their land. May was amazed that Ed seemed to be able to tackle any project.

They settled into planting crops and May worked in the vegetable garden. Little Freddie was easy to care for running around barefoot talking to the bugs and insects that he found.

Alice managed to spend many visits with May. She confided that she was pregnant and glowed with pride.

"Oh May, how is it that life can be so dark at times and then turn around and be so good!" Alice looked up to the blue sky with wispy clouds circling past.

"Yes you never know what the Lord has in store for you," as long as we help ourselves and each other the best we can, and make the rest up in faith." May thoughtfully conjectured. "Then we know that we lived life the way the Lord wants us to."

"By the middle of summer May knew she was going to add

to the family too. She and Alice had their heads together in the garden many afternoons discussing how their children would play together. They were thrilled to share in carrying the next life.

Ed was pleased too, but had a new concern.

COLONY PROBLEMS

It seemed that the Chicago-Colorado Company was failing. It was already having trouble in the spring of 1872 meeting the obligation of the paying the railroad for the land, and meeting the needs of irrigation for the farms. Costs of establishing the colony such as hauling drinking water and timber were higher than they anticipated. There were 500 members signed up. However, it didn't fail at that time, and we will never know what happened to help them out of the fix because the records were all burned during the 1878 fire at the newspaper office. The colony did survive until the lease ran out in 1883, and the town was incorporated shortly after.

It became clear to Ed that the Colorado Colony would never gain title for his land from the Railroad because they were not able to 'improve' the land in the desired amount of time, and that homesteading on the property would be pointless. Just as they were getting started, it seemed he had to do a complete turn around. and May was just beginning to feel settled.

"We'll have to return to Longmont for the winter I'm afraid, May," said Ed. "We can't sell the land because the title is worthless. The Colony will have to make good on their promise and trade back the land and swap it for another house in Longmont," he conjectured.

"Back to Longmont then?" May faced him. "It would be easier to be in town over the winter especially as the baby will be coming then," she agreed.

Ed nodded his head, "We'll find a little bigger place in town." He felt like all his efforts on improving the land were in vain. How lucky he was to have a wife who seemed undaunted by changing places. He gave her a reassuring hug and went to entertain Freddy as May prepared supper.

The Colony took the land back and swapped for a bigger house in Longmont. They were able to save and sell whatever crops Ed and May had planted. It was going to be a long winter and May was glad to be in town close to everything and everyone. She had brought the produce from her garden and could get fresh eggs and meat in town. The house had two bedrooms although small, Freddie could have his own space. May was content to watch him grow and her next one growing inside. She was looking forward to having a second baby.

ALICE'S BABY FRANKIE

Meanwhile Alice was due to have her baby, and May prayed for a healthy strong baby this time. When Isaac came into town to get the doctor, May was alerted and went to stay a few days to help Alice at their ranch.

"What a fine baby boy!" exclaimed May. Alice was blissfully looking at every finger and toe.

"We are going to name him Frank," Alice whispered sweetly. Alice turned to Isaac and smiled. He smiled back proudly and lovingly.

May did some baking for Alice in the large kitchen, turning out some bread and rolls. The stew was simmering on the stove giving a hearty smell and warming the cabin in the cold weather.

Alice slept until the wee cries of Frankie woke her to nurse him. May sighed and thought how wonderful that Alice was so happy. They were both blessed with wonderful husbands and new families.

Winter seemed to drag along. May kept busy sewing while Ed was away hauling hay with Isaac up to Georgetown in the mountains in the mining area.

1873
MAY'S BABY EDDIE AND GRASSHOPPERS

Edmond Rensselaer Jr. was born January 31, 1873 in Longmont. The doctor said everything went fine. Alice came with little Frankie to help out. She kept everyone fed until May was back on her feet. Ed was a wonder with Freddie while the women cared for their babies.

That spring Ed rented a place outside of town from Dr. Goodwin to grow potatoes. They had had such troubles with the grasshoppers last year and the year before eating the wheat, that he decided perhaps potatoes would do better. It seemed the grasshoppers leave their eggs in the ground which hatch the following spring and again for the fall. Farmers would have the most beautiful looking crops only to have them ravaged by the grasshoppers just as they were ready for harvest. The grasshoppers did indeed come again and ate all the grain, but only at the tops of the potato plants, leaving the tubers safe underground. Unfortunately though, the grasshoppers loved onions and would zone in on them and descend to feast until all were gone. Then what a smell would arise. The grasshoppers would get so thick that they would even interfere with the trains as they warmed themselves on the tracks creating a slippery mess for the trains when they tried to stop.

The area was opening to all kinds of people, Scottish, German, English, hunters, tourists and even city folks looking for the famous healthy air which was rumored to cure almost any ailment. The mountains beyond Longmont to the west were a constant invitation for exploration and wonder. A settler had founded a town called Estes Park, high in the mountains. Estes Park was named after the original settler Joel Estes and was ideal for hunting wild animals and fishing. Surrounded by the mountains, and fed by mountain streams, he deemed it a perfect idyllic place to raise cattle. His ranch was sold to Griffen Evans; and a few more homesteaders settled there and started ranching. It wasn't long before it became a popular place to vacation and camp for those living on the plains and travelers seeking the purported health benefits of its clear air and altitude.

One such traveler from England named Isabella Byrd, wrote about the area in letters to her sister. Her letters were published in book form in 1879-1890, *Life in the Rocky Mountains.* She stopped in Longmont to gather supplies and a horse to take her into the mountains. She wrote:

This is the Chicago Colony and it is said to be prospering, after some preliminary land swindles. It's as uninviting as fort Collins. We first came upon dust-colored frame houses set down at intervals on the dust buff plain, each with its dusty wheat of barley field adjacent, the crop, not the product of the rains of heaven, but of the muddy overflow of "Irrigation Ditch no. 2." Then comes a road made up of many converging wagon tracks, which stiffen into a wide straggling street, in which flaring frame houses and a few shops stand opposite to each other. A two-story house, one of the whitest and most glaring and without a veranda like all the others, is the St. Vrain hotel, called after the St. Vrain River, out of which the ditch is taken which enables Longmont to exist. Everything was broiling in the heat of the slanting sun which all day long had been beating on the unshaded wooden rooms. The heat within was more sickening than outside, and black flies covered everything, one's face included. We all sat fighting the flies in my bedroom, which was cooler than elsewhere, till a glorious sunset over the Rocky Range, some ten miles off, compelled us to go out and enjoy it.

A Sketch by A.E. Mathews in 1873 of Longmont
100 Years 1871–1971 Longmont Colony Centenial Then And Now
Longmont Public Library

IRRIGATION ST. VRAIN

Ed was upset about the grasshoppers, and bought 80 acres of land under irrigation near Isaac Richardson's ranch in the lower St. Vrain which was west of Longmont. He teamed and fenced and put in a crop. The family moved to the homestead there and May and Alice were neighbors at last. They helped each other with their families and enjoyed getting together in the evenings.

While in Longmont they were acquainted with one of the settlers, a Congregational minister Reverend Beech who bought the land next to Ed's. They tried working together for fencing and digging ditches for irrigation. Rev. Beech did not do his share of the fencing and failed to get his ditches ready for water.

One afternoon May and Alice had combined their supper for an evening together. Ed arrived at Isaacs and hailed him with a hasty greeting. The sun was still shining on the mountains and a warm breeze crossed the dusty corral. Ed quickly tied his horse.

"Whew what a time I'm having with Beech. He's proving to be a poor farmer and an angry neighbor." Ed confided in Isaac, "I can't help it if he's behind in his work, I've done all I can to help, he's just lazy and sore."

"Well, if you can't get your irrigation on now that your wheat is in, you won't get a crop," offered Isaac which didn't help Ed's frame of mind.

"I think I'll just turn the water on anyway, my ditches are ready, he'll have to deal with the fact that he has no water, I can't wait all season," steamed Ed. He splashed the wash water on his face and hands to get ready for supper.

Sitting down to dinner with the family, Isaac said the grace and they ate fresh fish, potatoes, and vegetables from the garden.

Isaac had some cows and they enjoyed milk, and butter that Alice had made, on the bread that May had baked. The women were absorbed with the children. Little Eddie was such a good baby, they didn't hear crying from him. But Frankie was always trying to climb on Freddie who was the oldest and he protested. The mothers then gave the babies a sponge bath and settled them to sleep.

"May, did you read in Nettie's last letter that Theodore sold their ranch? Do you think that they might come for a visit?" asked Alice.

"That would be nice. I was hoping Rensselaer would come too," answered May.

"Well at least he visited Nettie and Dora and read our letters," added Alice. "I'm glad he's working for the *Register* and not traveling around doing nothing." Alice laughed and they joined the men on the porch.

The parents sat on the porch and watched the night sky darken and bring the stars out. It was clear and the stars seemed to twinkle like diamonds.

When Ed turned the water on, Rev. Beech was so sore he shut off the water to Ed's ditches and turned it into the road. Ed was furious and couldn't get Beech to agree to anything. They finally submitted their case to court and hoped for a fair settlement by the arbitrators. To make things worse, the grasshoppers came again that year and ruined more than half of Ed's crops. The decision from the courts finally came and it ordered Ed to give Rev. Beech half of the remaining crop. Of course Ed thought it was unjust but he abided by the ruling. Ed found out later that the third member of the court was marrying a young girl who was living with Beech at the time. When half the remaining crop was taken to the threshers for Rev. Beech, Ed was determined to get away from him and considered moving back to Longmont.

Rensselaer's letter to sisters, July 27, 1873

At Home, July 27, 1873.

Dearest Sisters,

Nettie has just finished a long letter to you and I feel it is my duty to write a few words. I was at home last Sunday when Nettie read to me the letters she had lately received from you and how glad I am to know you are both well and getting along nicely. I am employed on the Register and will send you out a copy weekly. I will write you a letter soon. Hoping this will find you well.

I will remain your unworthy brother, Rensselaer.
Remember me to all.

Alice's letter to Ma, Sister & Brothers, Jan. 24, 1874

At Home St. Vrain Canyon, Jan. 24, 1874

My dear Ma, Sister and Brothers.

I have forgotten who wrote last but I guess it makes no difference as this is a lonely, warm Sabbath afternoon I cannot think of anything else to do, I must write to pass the time away. Isaac is taking a nap and Frankie is sitting on the floor by me looking at has picture book so you see that we are all well here. We are very comfortably fixed and have not suffered either from the cold or hunger but hard times keep us at home. Everybody says money never was so scarce in this country as at present. There seems to be a loud complaint among the farmers yet I don't see but everybody has enough and some to spare. We have just sold the last of our hay, of which we realized 30 dollars per ton on an average. Our ranch (farms are all called ranches in this country) is what is called a hay ranch out of our 80 acres we can only plow or raise grain on about 15 or 20 acres. Hay is the crop, it pays best, least work and surest crop. We have about 45 ton every year but as we hire it out we get half and expenses paid. Ed Lyman had it last year farther down the creek wheat pays best. Ed and May are now living in town but expect to move out on their ranch 10 miles east of town next month, then we will be twenty miles apart. Oh, dear, how I dread it. Isaac and I went down to Longmont a week ago yesterday. May and the babies were well. She has the sweetest little baby Eddie I ever saw, looks just like her, her ways and actions. He just begins to run along and you know how sweet babies are at that age. May does all her own work and cares for the babies a neater little housekeeper you never saw. Things go like clock work in her house while Ed thinks the "sun rises and sets" in her. Their home is a perfect model. Dora and Nettie, we have been looking for you ever since we heard you had sold out. What are you doing, or going to do? We wish you would come out. Ma., Frankie and all, I know you could do well and would like it. Come and Try. Well, Isaac says it is supper time so I will close. We are looking for Ed and May this evening. Frankie is a real chatterbox, he is trying to get up in my lap to "write to Gamma too" he says. He sends kisses and "ittle Pearl" his white calf, so when you see such things coming think of the sender.

I must not forget to tell you about my nice lot of butter I am making. We only milk two cows this winter and besides using all the milk and cream we need I make about 6 lbs. a week. I sell 5 of this for 45 and 50 cents per lb. It is my first effort and I feel quite proud of it. Now do write soon somebody or all, and let us know when to expect you. What would I not give to see Ma once more, but love to all and write soon. . Address us at Pella, Boulder Co., Colorado.

No news of Rensselaer yet.

Mrs. Alice Richardson.

1874
VACATION IN ESTES PARK

Despite May's protests to stay near Alice, Ed was determined to start fresh somewhere far away from Rev. Beech. Ed found a ranch 10 miles east of Longmont to rent where he could get out of the crop business and into raising cows and growing hay, which seemed a safer enterprise.

"I know that its going to be harder for you to be away from Alice, but how could we possibly stay with the state of things now with Rev. Beech." Ed pleaded with May. "If we can get ourselves in a good situation, perhaps you and Alice could have some extra time to visit, or even take a vacation to the mountains? I hear that settlers in Estes Park are welcoming tourists now besides the hunters and fishermen. You could go with Alice for a short trip during the summer now that the boys are a good age for traveling," he suggested.

"Oh that would be nice," May's spirits picked up a bit. She just wished that they could have a place of their own and finally settle down.

After moving to the ranch May concentrated on the boys schooling. Freddie was four and learning the alphabet and some words from his picture book. Eddie mimicked his brother and learned some songs while clapping his hands. The boys did some chores, sorting out the potatoes, and soaking the cabbage in vinegar to make sauerkraut.

Soon it was time to put in the vegetable garden and they helped plant the beans, peas, squash, onions, lettuce, beets and the potatoes that had sprouted over the winter. May was always happy in the garden with her boys. The morning sickness heralded the start of another child.

By July May was feeling better and had planned with Alice to vacation in the mountains. The road to Estes park had been improved and there were cabins to rent. The carriage ride was inexpensive and Alice and May were excited to see the mountains. They and the children climbed in the rig with their few supplies and the driver started the horses up the steep terrain. Ed waved good-bye and returned to Longmont with the wagon. He and Isaac were doing the haying while the women took a well needed rest from the daily chores.

Alice and May marveled at the steep canyon walls as they traveled beside the St. Vrain river that threaded through the mountain pass. The road then veered up through the foothills and they were surrounded by rocky terrain. One sheer mass of rock and mountain ahead of them slanted out of the earth like a brick red wall uplifted out of the ground. May and Alice were delighted by the magnificence of the formations and spent their time pointing and looking with the boys. At one especially steep grade in the road the driver asked the women to get out and walk so he could lead the horses beyond to better ground. Eddie cried when he saw his mother walking behind the carriage, so Alice carried him for May. The flowers were so beautiful. It was as if they had waited all winter to thrust up out of the soil to show their beauty. As the road leveled off they climbed back in to ride the rest of the way through the meadows of heavenly colors. The peaks of the farther mountains were just visible above the pine trees until they turned a corner and the valley panorama opened before them surrounded by majestic hills and white crusted mountains. The entrance to Estes Park was so spectacular looking down into the lush valley with the Big Thompson River meandering through it, that it took their breath away.

Alice gasps, "Oh, this is magnificent! What a paradise."

May could hardly believe her eyes. She braced herself for the descent and soon the carriage crossed the part of the valley towards the cabins that Mr. Griff Evans had for rent. Mr. Evans was a Welsh man with a younger wife and several children who had been known to have been living there since 1866. An avid hunter and fishermen he would sell his catch in Longmont and Denver. He also owned 1000 head of cattle which he grazed in Estes valley, and 50 horses for working his farm and for visitors to ride. When tourists started to come to the park, Mr. Evans built a few rustic cabins which he rented for $8 a week to families and travelers to enjoy. Mr. Evan's wife welcomed their guests at their table as well, continuing their Welsh tradition of singing and playing music after dinner. Their children ranged in age from four to a girl of seventeen. How welcome the family made May and Alice feel, and the young children were close enough in age to play well together.

May and Alice inspected the cabin and got the children settled inside spreading the hay for beds in the main room. The one bedroom Alice and May would share. Mrs. Evans invited them to tea and supper down at the main house for their first night, and May and Alice were very happy to not have to cook after their journey. They washed up with the pitcher of fresh clear water and took their meal of venison and shepherds pie under the trees with a group of other campers and the Evans family.

May complemented Mrs. Evans, "How lovely of you to put up with people constantly staying with you!"

"Oh, we enjoy meeting families, and hunters, and various people seeking a location that's good for the health and spirit. We like to keep up with what is going on in the outside world," Mrs Evans returned. "Besides I have to cook for the family anyway and the summer brings a good garden. Griff provides plenty of meat and fish."

The children gathered around their mother. Little by little they became curious of the three boys and before long they were racing about the yard. The oldest daughter helped her mother.

"I'm sorry that my husband Griff isn't here, he's at Ft Collins at a hearing about the shooting of Rocky Mountain Jim," explained Mrs. Evans.

"I'm sure everything will go well for him," May returned.

The subject was not spoken of again. The Women were not afraid of staying alone. It was common for their husbands to leave weeks at a time to do their work. Later during the week Griff arrived back at the Ranch and they found out that the case wasn't to be tried until July of the next year.

Entrance to Estes Park - Picture from: Estes Park Museum Friends Press, *Tracks in Time, A Children's History of Estes Park*

ROCKY MOUNTAIN JIM

Some of the local talk in the summer of 1874 was of the shooting on June 19th of that year of trapper Jim Nugent called Rocky Mountain Jim. He had been living in Muggins Gulch near the entrance of Estes Park. The year before he had been attacked by a bear which had left half of his face ripped up without an eye. However even the English Lady Isabella Bird had found him attractive and wrote about how genteel he was when accompanying her on rides in the mountains in the fall of 1873. Rocky Mountain Jim was known for past shooting escapades and had a reputation of drinking too much and getting wild and ugly. He and Griff Evans didn't see eye to eye on a lot of things. Also everyone in Estes Park was on edge about Lord Dunraven's trying to buy out the ranches of the settlers there to make the area a private game preserve. A Lord Haigh was sent from England to manage Lord Dunraven's affairs.

Abner Sprague a new settler to Estes Park, writing his account of the shooting from an eye witness, a one William Brown who had accompanied Jim, told the story: Lord Haigh had hired Jim Nugent for $100. to bring a woman acquaintance from Denver to Lord Haigh. But after a week and a half returning without the woman or the money, Lord Haigh accused him of being a thief and a liar. Mountain Jim forced him to take back what he said at the point of a gun to his head. So Lord Haigh was in fear of his life.

It had been known also on several occasions that Mountain Jim had threatened to shoot Griff Evans. On Jun 19, 1874, Lord Haigh was with Evans at his cabin at the Evans ranch when they saw Jim, with William, approaching on his horse with his gun ready. They suspected he was going to carry out his threats. Haigh went into the cabin to get his gun and prompted Evans to shoot. A couple of shots rang out; the first one missed Jim but hit the horse, the other wounded Jim after falling off his horse. Abner Sprague further explained how a piece of buckshot ricocheted off a wagon wheel or an object and hit Jim at the base of his skull.

Jim didn't die until three months later in September. Griff Evans turned himself in at the FT. Collins District Court and was accused at the preliminary hearing July 15th of firing a weapon with intent to kill. The case wasn't trialed until the following July 15th 1875. Evans was freed on bail until the trial, and Lord Haigh left the country.

Colorado was still a wild country where a lot of the disputes were often settled with a gun. The court system was trying to bring justice to the area especially with the Indian affairs. It was common to read colorful accounts in the newspaper of various shootings.

As promised Ed and Isaac arrived on horseback at Estes Park to share a few days enjoying the area with their families. They had never seen so many fish and Isaac shot a deer. They spent the remainder of the week hiking and fishing. Alice did some riding.

In the evenings they sang and swapped stories with the Evans family. They made a harmonious family time with *D'ye Ken John Peel,' Old Lang Syne, John Brown* and others. They talked of the dairy, the cattle, the crops which seemed to always be consumed by the grasshoppers and the local matters of interest.

LORD DUNRAVEN

A lot of the local talk was of Lord Dunraven, a descendant of the monarch of Ireland from the 3rd. century. He had been to Estes Park earlier during a hunting expedition and was in the process of buying the land in Estes Park to make a private hunting preserve.

The few settlers who were there were not selling out. He made up invalid land claims applications and made claims to more property than he was entitled to. He also bought some of the railroad land interest in the area. The British Lord was trying to turn the whole beautiful area into his own private estate. Political pressure was being brought to the local and state governments, and the government in Washington, to stop him from doing it. The governments were putting as many obstacles in his way as they could. Lord Dunraven had kept half the original land claims, some 15,000 acres. He was growing prized cattle and built a hotel in 1876. His mismanagement plus the agitation he received made him distressed and he finally turned his interest over to a stock company and left the area in 1878.

The last day of their vacation Ed started thinking out loud, "The railroad goes all the way to San Francisco, that sounds like a chance to get away from the feasting hordes. We could grow fruit!"

"Yes, peaches and apples!" blurted May. "But for now I guess we will be happy with the blueberries," May laughed as she wiped the blue lips of the boys picking from the low bushes. "The last time I had a good orange was in Garnett with Aunt Delia, I wonder how she is getting along; and little Media, I bet she is a grown woman by now."

"May, why don't we invite Media to come and stay with us, she would be a big help to you over the winter. She must be 18 by now, I think she would love to come and see you, it's been so long," suggested Ed.

May gave Ed a look of surprise and love for suggesting such an idea. "Yes! Since Aunt Delia sold the newspaper business and remarried, Media would be sure to have the opportunity to come. I did hope that Frank would be able to come, but Media will be perfect." With winter and the baby coming along, and Alice so far away, she would certainly need the extra help.

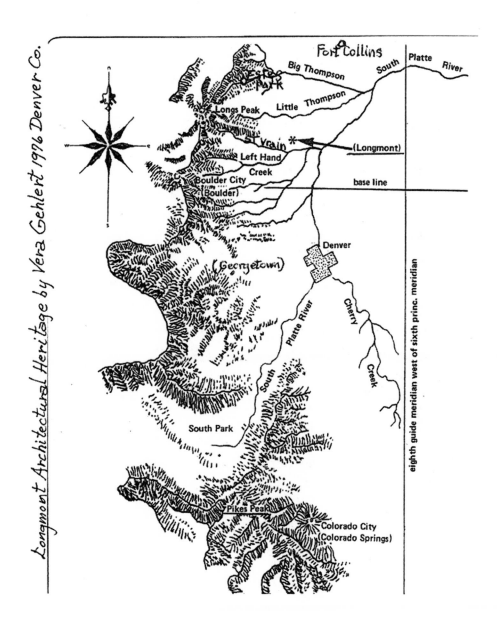

Longmont Architectural Heritage by Vera Gehlert 1996 Denver Co.

Fort Collins

Big Thompson

South Platte River

Park

Longs Peak

Little Thompson

Vrain * (Longmont)

Left Hand

Creek

Boulder City
(Boulder)

base line

Denver

(Georgetown)

Cherry

Platte River

South

Creek

South Park

eighth guide meridian west of sixth princ. meridian

Pikes Peak

Colorado City
(Colorado Springs)

Once back on the ranch, Ed realized they would have to add to their income to get through the winter. Only the second crop of hay had been spared by the grasshoppers.

By September when Media arrived, he approached May, "Since the crop didn't turn out as expected, there isn't any money coming in for the winter." Ed carefully chose his words, "would you mind if we took in some boarders to make ends meet?" He looked at her backside as she was busy washing the beets.

May turned toward him, her belly already swelling with her next baby, "That means more work, washing and cooking. Do you think it would bring in that much more?" She put the beets to boil on the wood stove.

Ed replied cautiously, "There's three extra bedrooms upstairs, besides Medias, that would be the maximum. We'd have the room downstairs and the boys would fit in the storage room together. The kitchen is large enough and we could feed everyone in the sitting room. I just have to make a table to accommodate everyone."

Ed felt he had solved the dilemma. Only a few cows were milking, but he calculated it would be enough to feed some extra people. Thank goodness for Media. She was a strong and able girl and helped Ed feeding and milking the cows.

"Well it sounds like you have it already figured out Ed," May laughed as she turned to him. "You are probably right, and we could do with the additional income. I'll set the rooms up and put an inquiry down at the store."

MAY'S LETTER TO MOTHER AND FRANK NOV. 1, 1874

St. Vrain, Nov. 1, 1874. Sunday evening.

My dear neglected mother I am really ashamed to think that it has been over two months since your kind and welcome letter came to hand and is still unanswered, but if you knew how many times I think of you and long to see you. I think you would not be angry at my neglect. The only reason I do not write oftener is because every day in the week, Sunday included, brings so many duties for me to perform for the various ones around me that I can find no time for outside social duties. This has been the busiest fall of my life, and if I did not have the best husband in the world to help me bear my burdens, I think sometimes I should give up and play sick. Since I last wrote, we have made some change in our circumstances. Last spring we moved on our homestead and Mr. Lyman fenced it and put in his crops. The dry season and the grasshoppers took all we might have raised and he got a good chance to sell out, so he sold land and improvements and invested in stock, mostly cows. He thinks that by renting a good hay ranch for a few years and putting all he can make into cows (aside from our living, of course) he will make more in the end, besides not working so hard. This is certainly the country for dairying and hay always brings a good price. Of course he would have to do most of the work in the dairy, but that is a very profitable business in Colorado. The ranch he has rented for the coming year is a real good one and he gets half of all he can raise and furnishes nothing but his work. We have the use of a house, barns, corral etc. and there is a good well and milk house. We shall take possession this week. The last month we have been living in a house where I have had to have three men to board, but from now on we shall be alone. If my health was better I would not mind the work, but I am far from being well and strong and cannot do as much as my ambition prompts me to do. Our boys are well, great big strong fellows as merry and good natured as crickets. Freddy, the eldest, now nearly four years old is the image of this father, but Eddie, who will be two in January, is more like me and our folks in looks and disposition. I really wish you could see them. I do wish you would send me your picture and the rest of the family, too. The trunk I lost in Missouri contained your picture, Frankie's and Willies and Pa's, so all I have of the family is Nettie's and Dora's. If I had the money I would be glad to pay the cost of having them all taken. I made Alice a short visit last month. She seems very happy and contented. She has a good home and a husband who loves her dearly and does all he can to make her happy. We never hear from Rensselaer any more and I fear we never shall. But there is no use for us to worry for he is in the hands of One who cares for us all, And it is a comfort to know that He never makes mistakes in His dealings with us all. Please write often and don't feel hard if I don't always answer soon, for I love you all and will write as often as I can. I think of you every day and wish I could see you.

May

St. Vrain, Colo. Nov. 1st, 1874.

Dear brother Frank.

As I am writing to Ma and it is not very late yet, I will write a little in answer to your letter which was received so long ago. I love to get your letters and wish you would write more often. It seems so strange to think that you are almost a man. It makes me feel old for it seems so short a time since I held you in my arms. But here I am, past twenty-four, five years a wife nearly. I am glad you stay at home and are learning to make yourself of some use in the world. So many young men never learn a trade and just float around perfectly useless and miserable. If you only start out in life with an aim and keep it in view and work up to it, you will surely come out conqueror. Above all things Don't enslave yourself with foolish habits of smoking, chewing, drinking or swearing. Keep your body pure and your mind will learn to keep itself pure if you avoid evil associates. You speak of coming west and if ever you should, of course my home will be free to you as a home. This is a pretty rough country for boys and a young man has to carry a stiff upper lip to get along. I like the country and have no desire to leave it. I think the climate and scenery cannot be excelled and a person stands as good a chance of getting a living here as anywhere. Of course there are drawbacks to any country and one who comes here expecting to find Paradise will be apt to go away disappointed. One must work here and learn to economize just as much as in the east. I wish you could come out just to try the country and climate. We have had most beautiful weather this Fall-cold nights but still, clear, warm days and no snow yet. The range has been white with snow ever since Sept. 1st and it looks beautiful to see the valleys and lower ranges clothed in a soft purple Indian summer haze while the higher ranges stand out so clear and white against the blue sky. If I had the time I would like to sit for hours with a spy glass or without and take views, it is better than any stereoscope. Well, perhaps you will see it for yourself some day. But it is getting late and I have already written a long letter, so I think it is time to close. Write often and tell me all about all my old friends. I hear from Uncle Lawrence's folks occasionally. They live at Union City, Mich.

Mr. Johnson writes to me quite often. He sent me two barrels of apples this fall. There is no fruit raised here or not much. Most of the fruit here comes from California and of course is very dear. I have not had a fresh peach for several years.

With love to Willie, Cora and all I sign myself as ever,

Your sister Mary.

Address Mrs. Edmund Lyman, St. Vrain, Weld. Co. Colorado, care of A. McKissick.

View of Longs Peak from Longmont, photo by June Morse

1875
MAY'S BABY JESSIE MAY

The winter of 1875 proved to be very cold in the minus degrees. May caught a bad cold with a cough and fever, and spent the month of December in bed with Media taking over running the house. Alice arrived to nurse her back to health. May was grateful for her company and feared for the child she was carrying, as well as being strong enough to get through the birth.

"I'm going to make you a mustard plaster to get rid of your cough," Alice bustled into the kitchen and prepared a soft cloth with boiling water and spread it with dry mustard. She secured it around May's neck and chest and tucked it all around. "There, that should drive out the mucus," she assured May. Just the moisture and heat was a relief to breathing.

Alice also made some peppermint tea. "Here drink this tea, May, it will help bring your fever down, even if you just sip a little bit at a time," she said as she propped May up with some pillows. Ed peered into the room, he was worried about May and the unborn baby.

Soup was always on the stove ready to be spooned into her mouth. May seemed to have lost track of time and talked in her sleep. Under Alice and Ed's care May slowly regained her strength. Ed and Media were careful to keep the boys from disturbing her. By January May was feeling better and on the first signs that her baby was on the way, Ed had the doctor there.

Little Jessie May was born January 12, 1875. May and Ed were so pleased with their darling girl and the brothers were gentle and talked sweetly to Jessie. Media was enthralled with the baby and helped May in the care. Alice came to see the baby and confided to May that she was going to have another child. They shared their joy and May promised to visit Alice in the spring. May showed her the pictures of their brother Frank and Willie that she received and Alice couldn't believe how Frank looked at 17 years old. How they missed their step mother's family.

MAY'S LETTER TO MOTHER, JAN. 27, 1875 - BABY JESSIE

St. Vrain, Colo., Jan. 27, 1875

My Dear Mother,

Suppose you are tired of hearing oft repeated apologies for not writing oftener to you so I will not say it all over again. Only this time I have a better excuse for negligence than ever before. I am sitting in the bright, warm sunshine which comes in at my bedroom window, too weak to sew, but feel in the humor for writing and guess you will not mind if do make a good many mistakes. I have been very sick since I last wrote and for a few days my feet came very near the Dark River which separates us from the other world. But God in His great wisdom and mercy saw fit to allow me to be spared to my loved ones for a while longer–no one can tell how long. On the 12 th. of Jan. at two o'clock in the afternoon a wee little daughter was added to our family. I had been sick for a month previous to her birth and was so weak and feeble that I never expected to live through it. But I have had all the care and attention that anyone could have and my strength is now coming back as fast as could be expected. The baby is perfectly sound and healthy and is growing finely. She has been very good so far. We call her Jessie May. Mr. Lyman is so proud and happy that I feel repaid for all I have suffered to give him his girl. I wish I could tell you what a good husband I have. He is so kind and thoughtful for my comfort, so patient and tender through sickness and takes the place of a mother to the little boys better than anyone else could. Little Freddie and Eddie are real well and very fond of their little sister of course. We have had very severe weather here this winter until about a week ago since which time we have had quite pleasant weather. There has been more snow than usual for this country and such cold weather has never been known here before. The day the baby was born was the coldest of the season. The thermometer stood at 36 degrees below zero all day. Mr. Lyman is wintering our stock down on the Platte River and so far they are doing very well. We talk of going to southern Colorado this spring or next Fall. We shall probably go to the San Juan country. I suppose you hear as much about the famine in Kansas and Nebraska as we do. There was enough raised in Colorado for everyone to live comfortably but times are very dull.

Mr. Lyman has not done anything this winter and we have to practice economy in every way possible. My cousin Media Olney, Uncle Isaac Olny's only daughter, came out from Kansas last fall and has been here all winter. She is a large strong girl, eighteen years old and she and Mr. Lyman do the work. We have had three boarders all winter so you see we have a house full. I thank you very much for the pictures of Willie and Frank. They are noble looking boys and I don't wonder you are so proud of them. I hope you will soon send the rest of the family as I am anxious to see you and your pretty little girl. If we can spare he money in the spring I mean to have pictures of our whole family taken. Alice made me a long visit in December. She is quite feeble this winter. She cried over Frank's picture for it seemed as if he had grown out of her remembrance. It seems so short a time since he was as small as my own little boys are now. I am anxious to have you see my family, for I am proud of them of course. Give my love to all –Nettie and Dora and I would like to have you or Frank write more often. I have been four days writing this letter for lack of strength. Your daughter, May

MAYS LETTER TO ALICE, FEB. 19, 1875- HEALTH

St. Vrain Feb. 19, 1875 At home Friday morning.

Dear Sister Alice.

We have not heard from you for a long time. Only once since you went away, but as I have a chance to send a letter out today I will write again. Mr and Mrs Scanton went away nearly two weeks ago. They started for southern Colorado but staid in Denver several days trying to sell a horse to raise money to go on, and finally rented a ranch three miles this side of the city, and have --letter damage-- and will probably stay there a year at least. I am glad they stopped there and it will be a nice place to stop when we go to Denver to trade. She left word for you to be sure to come and see her. I think they are very nice people and I shall enjoy going to see them. Media and I and the children are alone at present. Ed and Aaron started this morning to go down to look up the cattle. They may be gone two weeks, but if the stock is not too much scattered they will be back in a week. It will be very lonesome here while he is gone, for Media is away from home considerable. The young folks are preparing some exercises for the close of the school next week, and a grand entertainment the week after; It will consist of wax figures, tableaux, music & c., and Media takes quite an active part. So for me, I am able to be around and that is about all. My strength comes very slowly and I have the neuralgia and toothache so much that I am not able to do much more than take care of the baby, She is real good and grows finely. I hope to feel better when the weather settles. Just as soon as I am strong enough to stand the ride, I am coming up to see you. Media has promised to stay here and keep Freddie, for I would not think of piling our whole family on you when you are so feeble. I hope you are getting your sewing about done and hope I can help you. Try, if possible to manage your work so as to have nothing to do or worry about the last two or three weeks. If I had hired ten dollars worth of sewing don't last fall I would have saved money, for it has cost more than that for doctor bills and medicine not to speak of all I have suffered in mind and body. There was three days nights that I was so sick I thought there was no hope of my ever getting well, and I vowed then that if god spared my life I would never again risk it by trying to do more than two women ought to do. A mother has no right to throw away her health and strength, and I never shall again. If I can only be strong enough to take care of my children, I will let the work take care of it- self. You must take warning by my experience, and take better care of yourself. Let Isaac do your hard work, even if he don't do it just as nice as you would. He is able and willing, and it is better to have an untidy house than to leave your children motherless. I have learned this lesson by a terrible experience but I shall never forget it. Life is very dear to me for my husband and children's sakes and when I thought I was going to be taken away from them, I resolved to prize my treasures more and try to live for them as long as possible. Media has a very severe cold and is not able to do much. She will come and see you when it is convenient. She sends love to all. I want you to read this letter over many times, for I am afraid you are trying to do more than you ought to. Just remember that your own life and happiness and the health of your baby is concerned in the care you take of yourself from now on.

Kiss Frankie for me, and give my love to Isaac.

VISIT WITH ALICE BEFORE BABY

March came and with it news of Isaac selling his ranch and their family moving farther up into the mountains. May went for a visit to see Alice in their new house.

"Oh, Alice! This is beautiful looking out at the melting snow. You will never get tired of seeing this view," May exclaimed looking through the trees at the valley below to the east. All that could be seen of Longmont was a patchwork of fields and tiny buildings beyond. The prairie stretched out onto the snowy horizon like looking at the sea from up above on the shore. Eddie was playing games with Frankie and running around the house. May was trying to keep the peace since baby Jessie was napping.

"Yes May, I love it here. But now Isaac is talking about going to California," Alice sighed, "I wish it was easier to make a living here in Colorado, it's such a beautiful place to live." May looked at her with understanding, and smiled.

"It seems the Lord is out to test us. For as much and as hard as we work, it always seems like we are just hardly living. But you have made such a start here in the mountains, surely this healthy air will bring things around for you both," offered May

May's letter to Mother, May 2, 1875 - Grasshoppers

St. Vrain, Weld Co., Colo., May 2nd 1875.

My Dear Mother.

It has been so long since I last wrote you that I guess you think I am a very unreliable correspondent, but the time slips away so fast and every day is so filled up with its duties that I can hardly realize that winter has gone and summer come. We have had a cold winter, followed by a very backward Spring. The grass is just starting now and it looks no more like summer than it usually does the first of April. Farmers are about through with their crops or at least they are all waiting to see if the grasshoppers are going to take things before they put in any more grain. The grasshoppers that came last summer and took all the crops stayed long enough to lay the ground full of eggs and are hatching out now very thick. They have taken most of the wheat and oats throughout the country and will probably take everything before they are large enough to fly away. It is very discouraging to farmers, for losing the crops last year made hard times for everybody this winter. Mr. Lyman has gone down to get our cows. They wintered on the Platte river about thirty miles below here and he has been over a week already and will probably be gone a week longer. If he finds them all and they are in as good condition as we hope we can live this summer and fall on the proceeds of our dairy. We hope to have ten cows to milk this summer. We are trying to manage some way to buy stock enough to live on as farming is rather risky to depend on for a living. This soil and climate will produce fine crops if the grasshoppers don't come, but they have come nearly every year. I am getting quite well now although I am not nearly so strong as I once was. Baby Jessie is now nearly four months old and is a fine healthy baby. She is very small for her age but very pretty we think. She has long dark brown hair which curls all over her head and makes her look old. Large dark blue eyes and a sweet little mouth and chin. The little boys are very fond of her and help me considerably in taking care of her. Cousin Media Olney who stayed with me all winter is staying with Alice at present, but will spend the summer with me. I went up to Alice's and spent a week in March. She said she would write to you soon. Do you ever hear a word from or about Rensselaer? I am afraid he is dead for we cannot get any trace of him. I wish he had come out here two years ago. I shall expect to get yours and Cora's picture next time you write. I have our whole family except them and Pa's picture. Just as soon as we can spare the money I shall have the whole family taken for I want you to see them. Mr. Lyman often says he hopes to let me go back to Michigan in a year or two more and to Indiana for a visit. But we want to get settled in a home of our own before we do that. Alice's husband sold their place this spring for $1800 and he and Mr. Lyman talk some of going to California to make a home. But there is nothing certain about that yet. Give my love to Nettie and Dora and all the rest. Write often or have Frank do so.

Give him my love. Your daughter, May.

MAY'S LETTER TO MOTHER, MAY 24, 1875 - GRASSHOPPERS

May 24, 1875

Dear Mother.

You see the accompanying letter was written three weeks ago but I neglected to send it. Since it was written I have been up to see Alice again. I found her as well as usual. She expects to be sick before the first of June. She is real well and keeps a girl, so she has nothing to do or worry her. The grasshoppers have taken nearly every green thing in the valley. Thousands of acres of wheat came up only to be eaten as soon as it came. Many are putting in corn on their wheat ground but there is some prospect of more grasshoppers this fall. Alice and her husband are fully determined to go west next spring and we shall probably go with them either to Washington or Oregon or California.

Colorado is a splendid country for anyone who has money to buy a hay ranch or stock enough to live on. It is beautiful country and there is always a number one market in the mines for everything a farmer has to sell. But there is no vacant hay land to take up and we have not stock enough to keep us and there is no certainty of raising crops any year. So we think we can do better elsewhere. But there is nothing definite decided upon yet. I will write you again soon and let you know how Alice is getting along. Once more accept much love from us all. I tell my boys about you and Freddie often wishes he could go to see you. Please forgive my neglect and write soon.

Your Affectionate daughter, Mary Lyman.

May visited Alice once more before the baby was born, and she found Alice in good spirits. They planned another camping trip with the two families for that summer to go to Estes Park again. Media returned to Longmont with May since Alice had hired a local girl to work for her. May was cheered by her visit and sorely needed a distraction because the grasshoppers had come again that summer and devastated the early crop. Luckily May's garden was spared because she was late in putting it in.

MAY'S LETTER TO FRANK, JULY 4TH, 1875

Lower St. Vrain, Weld Co., Colo., July 4th 1875

Dear brother Frank

Your welcome letter was received about three weeks since and it is useless to say that I was glad to hear from you all. I am very glad to know that you are prospering and seemingly contented. We are all in excellent health. We are all right even if we are not making much headway in financial affairs. The summer is nearly half gone and yet we are having very cool weather and more rain than usual for this climate. Farmers have not had to irrigate near so much as last year. The grasshoppers left about the middle of June and there is more grain left than expected. We have saved only about four acres out of twenty six but some of our neighbors have saved a great deal more. If the hoppers do not come back this fall everyone will have a first rate crop of corn for it looks remarkably well now. Sunday, July 11, 1875. I commenced this letter last Sunday but was hindered and will now try to finish it. It rained nearly all of last week so the Fourth was rather a dull time. I suppose every one will have such a grand time next year that they did not care for this year so much. We intend to start to the mountains this week for a trip. We do not intend to be gone more than a week this time. I wish I live where you could take a trip with us to the mountains every summer. Do you ever think of coming west when you finally start out for yourself? We have talked some of trying Oregon or Washington but I am not willing to go farther west. I like Colorado and don't believe we shall ever find a country that has fewer drawbacks than this. For the past year we have not made anything on account of grasshoppers but I guess we will rent a ranch next year and try it again. When we can get about twenty good dairy cows we can do well to move into the mountains and give up farming. Here we have a healthy climate and scenery that can not be excelled elsewhere and when grasshoppers do not come, farmers can raise better crops and get a better price than in any of the eastern states. Alice was down here two weeks ago. She has another little boy nearly two months old now. She calls him Lawrence. She said she was going to write you and Ma soon. She and her family are going with us on our trip to the mountains. I was much disappointed in not receiving a picture of Ma and Cora in your last letter. I do want to see how Ma looks so much. Perhaps in my next letter I will send pictures of my family as I want to have them taken soon. Give my love to Nettie and Dora every time you see them. Please write to me often and tell me all about yourself and all the family and friends. As ever I remain you loving sister,

Mary G. Lyman

1875
CAMPING AT ESTES PARK

The two families packed the wagon with their camping gear and some provisions leaving some space for the children to sit with Media and Alice's girl Fannie. Ed hitched up his team of horses. They were all excited about camping and were talking about the fish they were going to catch. The three boys: Freddie - 4 ½, Frankie – almost 3, and Eddie – 2 ½, climbed into the wagon with the help of Media and Fannie.

Isaac was driving their team and carriage with May and Jessie – 6 months, and Alice with the baby Lawrence – 2 months.

The road had been improved and was much smoother with a way around the steep hills instead of getting out and walking up them. One of the settlers, Mr. McGreggor, was helping Lord Dunraven by trying to set up the road as a toll road. It would start the next summer, and was quite a topic of conversation.

Ed's wagon and Isaac's carriage went past the red uplift, through the foothills along the St Vrain River and into the rocky terrain. May was looking for the meadows filled with flowers and the snow capped mountain of Longs Peak. They had decided to camp closer to the base of Longs peak. When they descended into the valley of Estes Park with the Big Thompson River flowing through it, they came to the Evan's Ranch. Griff Evans came out to greet them. He had returned from the District Court at Ft. Collins.

"Howdy folks," hailed Griff. "Are you setting up camp this time?"

"Yes, we'll go a bit further near the base of Longs Peak," Ed answered. "How are you doing?"

"I just returned from the court trial and all charges were dropped against me. They decided that the shot that killed Rocky Mountain Jim was fired by Lord Haigh," laughed Griff knowing that he had left the year before.

"Well, now you're a free man you can count your blessings," Ed responded. He spoke to the horses and they continued on their way.

"Have a good time," Griff yelled after them.

The wagon turned on the less traveled path a little closer to Longs Peak. The meadows were covered with wild flowers and they chose a spot to camp with grass and only a few trees. After tending to the horses, Ed and Isaac set up the tent. The women miraculously made supper and fed the children.

A campfire was built and the smoke kept any mosquitoes away. Ed loved telling stories to the children and soon they were fast asleep. May and Alice nursed their babies to sleep. Alice knew that she would be awakened during the night for another feeding. May could finally sleep until day-break. Jessie was in that perfect baby time of sleeping through the night and not teething yet.

The men had more talk of Lord Dunraven and his plans to build a hotel.

"Next time we come to Estes Park we'll be able to stay at the Dunraven Hotel," chuckled Ed to Isaac.

"I'd rather sleep out in the clean air," retorted Isaac.

"Did you see his special high bred stock?" asked Ed.

"No, but I understand his brand is a fancy crown." Isaac lapsed into a careful study of the heavens starry creatures: the big and little bear, the snake, Orion's hunting belt, the seven sisters, and the brilliant milky way.

May considered the night noises of the crickets and the Whippor-will calling back and forth to its mate. An occasional coyote's scream rent the air. They gazed at the glow of the campfire and saw the fireflies thick over the meadow. This was a beautiful place to live.

Ed broke the silence. "If this next ranch doesn't pay off, I think we'll have to take the train to California and go to Oregon where's there's no grasshoppers. How about it Isaac, do you and Alice have a mind to go?"

"Well our mountain home is very pleasant, and working the cattle isn't that bad. We'll have to wait and see," Isaac replied. "Besides Alice has been trying to get her mother and family to visit," he added.

The rest of the week they fished and rode, then packed up for the long day trip back. May was facing another move to a bigger house belonging to Ira Lockhard who had taken quite an interest in Media.

MAY'S LETTER TO MOTHER, AUG.7, 1875 - MR. LOCKHARD

Lower St. Vrain, Colorado, August 7ᵗʰ, 1875

My dear mother;

It has not been long since I mailed a letter to Frank but as I am in the mood for writing today I will write a little to you. This warm bright Sabbath day finds us all in usual good health in the enjoyment of many of life's blessings with a reasonably good prospect of future prosperity. We have just been moving into another rented house where we my remain for two or three years. It is only two miles from where we rented last year so we are still in the same neighborhood.

This place belongs to a Mr. Lockard, an old settler in Colorado, and quite a wealthy bachelor. His ranch here is worth about twelve thousand dollars. The house is very large white frame, nicely finished and conveniently arranged. I have just bought me a new carpet, the first one I have ever had. It is a very pretty ingrain and I have my front room and bed room looking quite cozy and homelike. We are not milking any of our own cows now but will have three or four fresh ones this winter. Mr. Lyman will work here by the month until spring and then perhaps rent here next season if we do not go to Oregon. Mr. Lockard pays him thirty dollars a month and we are at no expense at all I keeping up the house, his wages are clear gain. We have been obliged to sell off some of our stock to live on this year, so we have only nine cows left besides a few calves. We did not like to sell it but it has always been our rule to keep clear of debt and as we raised nothing much last summer and I was sick nearly all winter it made rather hard times for awhile. But we hope now to be able to get ahead a little. I am not strong this summer and do not feel able to do much more than my sewing and take care of the baby Jessie. She is teething and quite restless. She is such a little tiny creature compared to what my boy babies were. Cousin Media is still with us and will probably remain here until she marries. She is so much help to me I could not get along without her. We all took a trip to the mountains in July. Alice and her family were with us. We went up St. Vrain canyon to Estes Park, a large and beautiful park situated just at the base of Long's peak and quite near the snowy range. The park contains two or three hundred acres of land and is well watered by several large streams of water and has several lovely little lakes in

*it. We fished, rode and walked for four days in the Park.
Trout is plenty there and I never saw such lovely flowers
anywhere as grew wild up there. You would be delighted
to see some of your choicest flowers growing wild in great
profusion..........*

MEDIA'S WEDDING

Media had met a wealthy bachelor, Ira Lockard, the man of her
dreams. He was attracted to her strength and ability to help run a
household. When she told him of the Lyman's interest in working
a ranch, he offered Ed a job at his ranch. There was a farmhouse on
the property for the help other than the main ranch house, which
would be perfect for them to live.

Mr. Lockard was interested in Media becoming his wife and this
would be a convenient situation for him. She would be close by
until the wedding and would live with him in the main house after
they were married.

May was particularly unhappy to lose Media, but was proud and
pleased with her choice.

The wedding plans proceeded. Ira's parents and his two brothers
came. Alice and Isaac's family, and a few of Ira's friends. Ira introduced his parents and brothers Bruce and William, and the other
guests.

It was a hot day and Media looked lovely in a short sleeved or-
ganza dress that May had sewn for her. May stood up for Media
wearing her white blouse and navy skirt, her regular church outfit.

Ed accompanied Media to the flowered arched trellis and felt
like a father putting her hand into Ira's. The pastor had them say
their vows and Bruce handed the ring to Ira. He gently slid it onto

Media's finger and the pastor pronounced them man and wife.

The repast of sandwiches and tea punch was set up outdoors as the sun's long shadows fell over the grass. Alice was impressed with Media's beautiful layered cake. Media had carefully made little pink roses on the white icing. She had also made little gifts of fruit cake and nuts. It was a lovely afternoon.

The bride and groom were planning to honeymoon in Denver soon before settling in the ranch house. The children all hugged and kissed Media who was glad they were going to be close neighbors.

ALICE'S LETTER TO FRANK, SEPT. 1875- INVITATION

Dear Brother Frank: I have just finished writing to Ma and have not said half I want to But I want her to come out here. This mountain air will do her so much good and I know she will enjoy herself so well. You and Willie are both young and can come anytime but ma has seen the most of her life and most of it has been spent right at hard work, she has done a great deal for us children, more than we ever know until we have children of our own and even then it takes a lifetime to find out. Now what have we done for her cannot the pleasures we have given her be counted? I think so Now I propose that each one of us children give her a little recreation. Now I live in a country where all the pleasure seekers of the world come and well they might for this is indeed God's own country. It's awfully grand mountains with their lakes and peaks some 10,000 ft higher than you are (there is Estes or Allens Peak higher than the mouth of the St. Vrain Canyon And that is just a mile higher than New York) by good authorities. So you can

Imagine the height from your place, perpetual snow is only five miles from Estes Park, but the climate in the Park is very pleasant, hundreds of tourists are visiting there every summer. May and I were there Late summer and Isaac and I are going again week after next to spend a week or two then after we get back we are going up to Caribou in Boulder Canyon, the highest town in the mountains, away up to the timber line, next to the snowy range. Now if Ma will come we will take pains to show her everything. We have a good team and know the way and it may be the last opportunity she may ever get with out it costing her all she is worth. We have a beautiful mountain home, the best of water and everything to make her comfortable. Now don't you or Nettie be selfish and say she can't come for she can surely ride on the cars and she will not have to change but once or twice anyway and then not change depots and we will meet her at the depot here. Now can't she come and if she regrets it she can return as soon as she wants to. I will tell you plainly what I will do that is husband and I want to know what you and Nettie will do. Of course we are not any of us rich but Ma and Corie can come out and return for less than a hundred dollars but the hundred will make her more comfortable and we will go half if you, Willie, Nettie and Dora will go half. Now is that not fair? For Ma's sake, but if you will not I will go all for the sake of the pleasure and benefit of health she will receive and I know she will never regret it. She need not go to any expense in getting ready. She will be just as welcome and Nettie can go and keep her house until her return. Now what in the world is to hinder her from coming right away. I want her to go to the Exposition in Denver with us in September where will be seen everything from Colorado, Utah, California and all the west that has been to the Centennial. Ma will see more and learn more at the world in two months time that she ever knew. Now don't refuse me this one favor. I would like to have Mr. Painter come too, he would be just as welcome but I suppose he never cares about us children. I hope he does and will come with Ma., he would enjoy the mines I am sure and we would do all we could to make it pleasant for him. I wish he would come. Our prospect for good crops never was better. There is nothing to prevent our success now unless the 'hoppers' come this fall. No one thinks they will. We spent our 4th upon a high mountain with a picnic and the country from Denver to Cheyenne could be seen. We watched the fireworks and it was the grandest sight I ever saw. There are no Indians nearer than Cheyenne and Ma need not be afraid because the people are coming all the time. I will send you some papers so you can see for yourselves. Oh how happy I will be if ma will only come. Cousin Media married a rich man and keeps her fine carriage and horses and lives only a visiting distance from here. Ma will love her I know.

As ever, Alice.

MAY'S LETTER TO ALICE OCT. 11, 1875

At Home Monday morning St Urain Col. Oct. 11, 1875

Dear Sister Alice

I have tried to find time to write to you for a week past but have failed to do so, and will take the time now. We are at leisure today, as the men are off threshing at the neighbors, and it is quite a treat to us to be alone. They are through haying but we will have four men to cook for still, for they are baling and hauling off hay all the time. We all keep pretty well and busy as ever. Media has not been to Denver yet but is going this week. She has just finished her dress and cloak. The dress looks very pretty indeed and is well made. She has got pretty tired of it, for it has taken so long to make it. She will get her a hat in Denver. I have not got anything yet for the winter only one everyday suit for the boys. Oh yes I forgot, I have a nice new dress. We traded our old cook stove to Mrs. Beach. She gave me two real nice new comforters a nice pair of blankets and a flannel sheet a nice dress pattern: it is all cashmere very soft and heavy. There is only four yards and a half in the piece but it is a good yard a half wide. I wish I had you here to tell me how to make it. I shall not make it up right away for it will cost considerable to get trimming for it, such as I want. It is cinnamon color. I went down to see Amanda Boyington's baby yesterday. She has a fine boy about a week old, she is getting along first rate.

Mrs. Dudley and her family have just started for the mountains. They are going to keep boarders where Mr Dudley is working. They may stay all winter. Ed spoke to

Mr. Mulverhill about renting his ranch for per ac. It is a splendid hay ranch, as good as this. A large white house and only about a mile from here. I wish you could get it. There is a man on it now but Mr. M did not know whether he would stay or not. There are other places near here just as good. Ed has the California fever as much or more than ever but if we can stay here a year or two we can better afford to go then now. Jessie is learning to creep but has no teeth yet. She weighs eighteen pounds.

Was up town last Saturday for the first time in two months and came home with the neuralgia. I am going to take Mrne Demorrest's magazine next year. Well I guess I have told all I know. I am anxious to hear from you. Has your friend Fannie gone yet? You must feel lonely when she is gone.

I can't tell when I can come to see you, but hope to before winter. Mr. Lockard will keep one man besides Ed all winter, so you see there is enough work to keep one at home. Are you going to have a machine this fall. It seems as if I must have one, but guess I can't. Good bye Love to all. Kiss the little one for me. Media says she will write you a long letter when she comes home from Denver. She sends love to all. Write to us soon.

Your loving sister May

Media says if her cape is left there by Mrs. Burnett to leave it at Gloyn store with her name on it, and if you will please send baby's hood with it. I will try to come and see you soon.

MAY'S LETTER TO FRANK OCT. 17, 1875- PICTURES

At Home, Sunday, Oct. 17, 1875.
Lower St. Vrain Colo.

Dear Brother Frank.

It has been a month since I received your welcome letter. I did not intend to neglect answering it so long but my excuse is a good one for I have so much to do that Sunday comes I feel so tired and weak that I can't write. But the haying season is over now and I shall not be quite so harried now. The lovely Indian summer is here again. To me the most beautiful season of the year. I love so well the long, quiet, hazy days when all nature is slowly changing its bright summer hues and preparing for coming storms and winter days.

We are all well, except colds. Our little girl is teething and consequently not very well, but grows finely and is as "pretty as a peach" her papa says and he thinks he knows. Tell ma I thank her very much for her and Cora's picture. Cora is a little beauty and I think Ma has reason to be proud of her present family. Ma has grown old since I saw her in her looks as well as years. How I do wish I was able to come and see her once and have a long visit. But in all human probability we shall never meet again in this world. In the Spring we intend to start for California. I rather dread to go so far, for I should never expect to come back. Yet we think we can do better and find a home that will satisfy us. I am so anxious to get a little home and settle down for life, and educate my children and make

119

them as happy and useful as possible. We intend to go in to Denver this Fall to some trading and I shall have our whole family's picture taken. I was so glad to hear from Rensselaer again. You did not tell me half enough about him. What is he doing, is he married, where is he going—why don't he write to me or come and see me. I guess he don't care much for me. Alice was visiting here when your letter came, she said she should write you very soon. If I knew Rensselaer's address I would write him a long letter, I really believe he has half forgotten he ever had a sister and I guess he don't know my name or address. The farmers are all busy gathering corn. There is a pretty good corn crop and an average crop of wheat and a first rate crop of grass. If we could only raise fruit here or buy it for a reasonable price I would not care to leave Colorado. But in California we can have fruit of all kinds and grasshoppers are unknown there. I guess there is nothing more of interest to add. Please write all you know about Rensselaer and send his address. Does he go by the name of Martin? Give my love to Nettie and Dora. Tell Ma I hope to send her my picture soon. Love to all,

Your sister Mary Lyman.
Address Longmont, Bolder Co., Colo.

MAY'S LETTER NOV 15. 1875
POLITENESS OF C. HOWARD – HAND DELIVERED

Nov. 15, 1875 Sunday night at home.

Dear Sister Alice

I thought some of coming up with Mr. Howard's but can not make arrangements to do so now, but shall come up just as soon as I can. I would give lots to see you tonight for I've got the blues. We can only stay here until the first of January – have not had any falling out, but Mr Lockhard has made arrangements different from what we were calculating on. Don't know yet what we shall do or where we shall put in our time from then till grass comes so we can start for California. Ed thinks he will come up and see Isaac about letting me live with you this winter and he work out. But we are unsettled in our mind at present and cannot tell just what will be the best for us to do. Please write and tell us when you are going to move up to Red Hill and what would be the chance for me and my chicks to crawl into one corner of your house until Spring. Have you sold your stove? Where are you going to spend Thanksgiving. Media is working at the Boyington's now but will come home after this week. She wants to come up to see you very much. We all keep pretty well. I have been having the rheumatism lately but feel well today. The weather is horrid. I am tired and nervous tonight and guess you think so by the looks of this. We want to go to Longmont tomorrow if it clears up. Love to all.

In Last your Sister May

CHRISTMAS TIME

1875 ALICE'S LETTER TO FRANK

Dearest brother Frank.

I have been writing to Ma and of course you will read it if it contains anything of interest to you, but you spoke in your letter that perhaps you might come out here next Fall. Oh how I do wish you would, I shall be so lonely after sister goes away. I don't know what do if you could only come this Spring before Mary gets away. If they should go by team, then I know you would be favorably impressed with one of the most beautiful countries that ever was. I also know that you could put in one year of pleasure and profit. I know the lessons of observation could pay you well for your trouble. I would like to go home next fall if we do well next summer and if I do could you not come home with me if you cannot come before. I should want you to promise not to leave home or Mo. for any length of time but we claim a good visit from you if Ma can spare you a year and I should be glad to see Willie too, although he has always been a stranger to us. I claim a share of friendship for Ma's sake. Well, Frank, I suppose you are sleigh riding now while we have no such pleasure here. I have not had a sleigh ride since I left Michigan nor seen snow. enough at any time, that is, it did not last more than a day or two at a time and as there are no sleighs in the country we could not enjoy what little snow there was. Game is very plenty this winter, the snow of the range has driven the deer, antelope, elk, bear, lion and several kinds that I am not familiar with down on the valley. Trout is also plenty up in the park. The young men of this neighborhood are getting ready now to go out on the plains on a Buffalo hunt. The holidays passed quiet with us. Christmas we got a pretty little pine tree and our hired man fixed himself up as Santa Claus and came in the front door with a few presents in a basket and put them on the tree and no you could not make our little boys believe but what it was the old man himself. A few of our neighbors came in and we popped corn and spent a very pleasant Christmas eve. Well, Frank, I wish all of your folks were gathered around our fireplace tonight. Mary is getting her baby girl asleep. Isaac is getting ours to sleep and Ed has our three little boys in one corner of the room telling them childish stories, each one listens with all eagerness and remembers all that is said. My little Frankie knows all of his letters and can read some, Freddie is learning his letters now. Dear little Cora, how I love to look at her picture. Is she as pretty as her picture? How much she and Willie look alike. How old is she? Can't she print a letter to Frankie and he will answer (through me) that will get them acquainted. I send much love to Nettie and Dora and wish they would write and I will write to Nettie if she will answer. I wish you would tell me how La Grange has changed, who lives in our old home, how does it look, where are all our acquaintances and the neighbors around the farm of Mr. Painter, who are left and where is Valentine Station. How does Nettie like City life and is Charlie Hoyt in Kendalville now. He was a printer. Where is Uncle William's people now do please answer the questions, Frank, and oblige your sisters here.

Alice

ALICE AND MAY'S LETTER TO MOTHER PAINTER - JAN. 2, 1876

Upper St. Vrain, Colorado.
Jan. 2nd, 1876

Dearest Ma,

I received your letter New Years eve and could not have asked for a present that suited me better. I send in return many thanks and will surely remember you when we have a good one taken. May and I both will have our families pictures taken for ourselves and friends before May starts for California which may be in the course of a month if Ed succeeds in selling his team. He will go this week to Denver to try. I can scarcely endure the thought of their going so soon but they think they must go and are anxious to be getting a home. They feel unsettled and Ed is very ambitious and with their little family they need a home. If Ed succeeds in selling his team they will go through by railroad. It will take six or seven days by rail, going night and day from Cheyenne and by team it will take two months or more from here besides having to wait here four months at least or until feed gets good. They will save time and perhaps a great deal of trouble to go by rail. How much I do wish we could go now but we will move on our mountain ranch in a week or two and stay there until we can sell and not sacrifice too much. We are doing well now and we have both learned in this world to let well enough alone. We have got 17 head of cattle, all cows but one, and 6 head of horses, two good work span of work horses and two valuable two year old colts besides chickens, ducks, pigs etc. got a large house and everything to do with both outdoors and in and of course if one wants to sell such things they must make a great sacrifice. We are not able to sacrifice so much just yet so we cannot tell yet when we will go. I expect, Ma. that you think California is almost out of the world and that if we get there we can never get home. To us it seems only a little ways and just as easy to go back home from there as here. If we do not go for a year or so I will come home to see you by next Fall. If we succeed in raising a good crop next summer nothing could please me more. Well, I will close for the present wishing you all a

Happy New Year. Alice

Dear Ma.

Alice has left this page for me to finish. She has said about all there is to say. We are enjoying these winter days together and it may be the last time we can ever be together. Our children, five in all, make a houseful but we get along first rate. We have not had much winter yet. All the month of December was warm and no storms at all. I feel sorry to go farther west without having a chance to come and see you but we think it is best at present and in time we may be able to meet again. I will be sure and have our family's pictures taken before we go and send you one. I will not fail to write often to you wherever I am and want you to do the same. With love to each one of your family, especially yourself, I remain, your loving daughter. Mary Lyman.

1876
CALIFORNIA AND OREGON

After Ed sold his team of horses in Denver, the family packed for their trip to California. They were driven to the train station at Platteville just outside of Longmont by Isaac who sent them on their way with well wishes for the journey. May and Alice had already said their good-byes and May hoped it wouldn't be too long before her sister and family would join them.

The train brought them north to Cheyenne, Nebraska where they changed trains to go West. When they got to Ogden, just north of Salt Lake City, they changed trains to an express train. It was dark and it was difficult moving the children since they had fallen asleep.

MAY'S LETTER TO ALICE, JAN.27, 1876- ON ROUTE

Wells, Nevada Terry.
Thursday, Jan. 27, 1876.

Dearest Sister:

Here we are 664 miles east from San Francisco. We change cars at Ogden last night just at dark and were put on the express train, thus making our journey two or three days shorter than it would have been on the emigrant. This morning at 4 o'clock we were stopped by a big snow drift and they took five engines and a snow plow to clear the track.

We were delayed five hours. It takes two engines to run a train there is so much snow.

The country here is wide vallies with mountains on all sides. We are now in Humboldt valley. There is no timber, low sage brush everywhere. Jessie was croupy last night and is real cross today. We are quite comfortably fixed. We shall be in the Sierra Nevada's tomorrow, then look out for snow. The weather is cold. May

MAY'S LETTER TO MOTHER PAINTER FEB 27, 1876- OREGON

Butteville, Marion Co., Oregon,
Sunday, February 27th, 1876.

My dear Mother;

We are away up here in Oregon more than three thousand miles from you; but I am thankful that we can write and thus make the distance shorter. I wrote to you just before we left Colorado and Alice said she would write to you. We took the cars at Platteville Colo. Jan, 24th and arrived in San Francisco the next Saturday early in the morning, thus being only five days and nights on the way. We had a very pleasant and safe journey and saw many wonderful sights along the way. In crossing the Sierra Nevada mountains we saw snow six feet deep on a level and the cars run through over fifty miles of snow sheds. We saw the Devil's Slide, Hell Gate, and all the beautiful scenery in Weber Canyon. We went around Cape Horn and it fairly made me tremble to see the cars go flying over what seemed to be such dangerous places. The road winds around so that sometimes the train seemed almost doubled. Some places they had to put on five engines and a huge snow plow to clear the snow from the track. It seemed strange to go out of such deep snow and cold weather right into California where the fields were green with grass and grain and flowers were blooming out of doors. We were delayed in San Francisco four days and while we were there we visited many parts of the city. We went to Woodwards Gardens, which is a large park enclosed by a hedge and containing more wonderful sights than I ever dreamed of. There is a large collection of animals of every kind from the huge elephant to the tiniest little mice. It would take a person a whole day just to see all the animals. Then there is a large Aquarium containing fish of every variety all swimming about in large glass cases. There are several large hot houses all made of glass where were seen all kinds of flowers and plants, beautifully arranged and with numerous little fountains tinkling among the flowers. Then there is the Art Gallery and the Music Hall, the Museum, and the main building which is up on a high hill and from the top of which we had a birds eye view of the whole city and the ocean in the distance.

But I cannot tell half we saw there. On our way back to our hotel we went by the grand Palace Hotel which is the largest hotel in the United States. It is seven stories high, covers four whole blocks and cost over seven million dollars. It is perfectly magnificent inside and outside. There are elevators to carry one from one story to another and it is beautifully lighted with gas all over and every room is furnished with great elegance. We saw so many Chinese in the city. Some of the rich ones live in grand style and dress very nicely in their native costume. On Wednesday morning Feb. 2nd, we got on board the steamship Ajax and started for Oregon. The bay was beautiful. I never saw sailing vessels before, and the scenery along the shore was fine. There are two large forts at the entrance of the bay and we went out the Golden Gate we saw large sea lions playing on the rocks. But as soon as we were on the ocean we began to grow sick and had to go to our rooms and did not leave our berths again for three days and nights. The ship rolled terribly and I was somewhat frightened, but on Saturday morning............ Tell Frank and Willie to get a map and find me. I am on the west bank of the Willamette river about half way between Portland and Salem............we left the ocean and entered the Columbia river. This is the a very large stream larger than the Missouri and there are many large salmon fisheries along its banks, Early Sunday morning we arrived in Portland. This is the most important town on the coast north of San Francisco. We had to stay there one day and night and early Monday morning we took the steamboat and came up to Butteville. We heard of several good farms to rent around there and Ed found us a good place to stay while he looked around. In a few days he had rented this place and we moved on it at once. We are only two miles from Butteville so that will be our address. If you look on a map you will see that the Willamette river runs almost through the state north and south, we are right on the bank of the river or nearly so and can see the steamboats almost every hour. Off in the north east we can see the top of Mount Hood. This is a timbered country, most of the trees are fir and cedar and grow very tall. It is a splendid farming country. Grain and vegetables grow in great abundance and of most excellent quality. As to fruit, it goes to waste for want of care. Apples, pears, plums, cherries and all kinds of small fruit grow in great quantities and the best quality. Peaches do not do as well as other

129

kinds of fruit but there is so much fruit that they are hardly missed. The climate is very mild From November till April there is a good deal of rain. It very seldom freezes or snows. The rest of the year it is warm and just rains enough to make everything grow. It is never very hot, on account of our nearness to the ocean. We are very much pleased with the country, judging from what we have seen and heard of it. We have rented this farm for two years, with the privilege of staying five year if we want to.

Mr. Graham, the owner, furnishes us a house and large garden, a team and feed for it and all the seed and we get half of everything on the farm. There are two good orchards. He keeps sheep and we get half of the lambs and half the wool. When we had got here and bought a stove and a few dishes and provisions we had just sixty-five cents left. So you see we are starting at the foot of the ladder again, but I have never felt more hopeful and ambitious in my life than I do this Spring. We have a little money yet to come to us from Colorado and that is all we have. But we are both young and strong and willing to work and economize and our children are all healthy and sound. We have always had enough to be comfortable and have always been happy. This is well settled country and has good schools and churches and I like the people we have met very much indeed. But I am tired of writing and will have to stop for this time. I had to write with a pencil for we have no ink. Give my love to Nettie and tell her this letter is for her and you too. I mean to write to her soon. Please write as often as convenient for now I am among strangers again and a letter from you always seems to carry me back to the old home. I meant to have had our pictures taken before this but we could not spare the means this winter. I look at your picture very often and wish I could see you. I have not heard from

Alice since I left her five weeks ago yesterday. I will write again soon.

Your affectionate daughter,

May G. Lyman.

May and Ed and their family of three children managed to travel through the mountains in the middle of winter. When they were in San Francisco staying at a hotel, Ed met some people who were going to Oregon. Even though they were planning to go to Santa Cruz just south of San Francisco because one of Media's friends family had settled there, it sounded more ideal for them to go to Oregon instead. Therefore Ed secured a passage on the steamer to Oregon.

After a pleasant departure the ocean waves made the whole family seasick and they spent the passage in their berths. How welcome the calm waters of the Columbia River and arriving in Portland were. Arriving in Portland they stumbled ashore to getting their sea legs under control. With renewed energy they took the smaller steamboat up the Willamette River to Butteville.

Once in Butteville Ed arranged with Wallace Graham to rent a house with a garden complete with a team and feed; and he would work at Mr. Graham's Hop-yard at Carter's Ferry for half the crop. When this didn't pay he rented One and one half acres from Mr. Graham to grow strawberries and vegetables. Berries were a lucrative crop.

June Morse sitting on the porch

Butteville Store, Butteville Oregon 2014 and Circa 1870

DEATH OF ALICE'S FRANKIE

Meanwhile May received a heart wrenching letter from Jimmy Wagoner a friend of Alice and Isaac. It said that Alice and Frankie had been sick and that little Frankie succumbed to the high fever and didn't recover. Alice was overwhelmed with grief. She could hardly bring herself to write to May. It was so sad after losing her firstborn with Mr. Hoyt, that to lose a healthy child almost 3 ½ years old was unbearable. May's sympathetic nature wrung itself out in her support for Alice.

Drawing of Steamboat Circa 1870 at Butteville Landing
Picture from Butteville Store Library at Butteville, Oregon

MAY'S LETTER TO ALICE, MARCH 20, 1876 - CONSOLATION

Butteville, Marion Co., Oregon.
March 20, 1876. Monday evening.

My darling sister,

I feel tonight as though I would give anything I possess to be with you and fold my arms around you and say nothing; but as that pleasure is denied me I must write. I received a letter from Jimmy Wagoner yesterday afternoon containing tidings of your terrible affliction. I was so stunned and bewildered I could do nothing all night but think of you and weep with you. I cannot realize it that our darling Frankie, the brightest flower in the whole family, had left us all and gone to bloom in another home. My precious sister, I wish I could say one word of comfort but I know that to you, words are hollow and in vain. I can only mingle my own tears with yours and try to say to your crushed and bleeding heart, "he is not lost, just gone before." Just a little longer to wait here and you too will pass the narrow stream that divides you from him, and you will meet your darling in the land where death never comes. God in his great love saw that his tender, sensitive, noble nature needed more congenial surroundings that it could have here and took him to eternal happiness before there was one stain on his pure little heart. I know you yearn for him every moment and feel that life is all a blank waste without him, for your love for him was more than common love, it was worship. But when I think of all he must have suffered had he lived, how harsh words and wicked deeds would have met him as he met the world. I say, or try to say "it is well as it is". And the most comforting thought of all is this, "it is only for a little while, in His own good time He will take us to our rest and home sweet home". You have some good works to do before you are free and you know your darling is safe from pain and sorrow, waiting for you and praying perhaps to have the angels leave the gates ajar so s you can catch a glimpse of him. I cannot tell you how my heart aches for you. It sometimes seems to me that all the good things come to me while all that is hard and bitter is given to you.

God Knows if I could bear some of your burdens for you I would do it gladly. Yours has been a life of bitter disappointments and keenest suffering, for you have such an intense nature that you cannot help giving your whole heart in love. But God pities you, I know, and in a little while longer you will be permitted to go where all wrongs will be righted and you will then have a just judgment which has been denied you here. It is better for your precious boy to go first than for you to go and leave him alone. You can bear the sorrow better than he could. I cannot bear to think that my little Frankie is gone, Only when I think that he is where all is love and peace and I and my little band will sometime go we shall know no more partings.

May's Letter to Alice, March, 1876

To Alice

We have been here now over six weeks and have not heard from anyone but Jimmy. And here let me put in a word for him. Tell him I thank him for his kind and gentlemanly manner of writing the sad news, and for his promptness in writing. I send him our best regards. He told me no particulars only that you had been sick and was then at Gold Hill. I am glad you have a friend Fannie to stay with. I am sure she will be a sister to you and I shall always love her memory for your sake. I want you to make up your mind to come out here just as soon as you can. What time we have to live may as well be spent together. And I need you and you need me.

We never met so many fine people in my life in so short a time as I have found here. They are all so kind and cordial and hospitable that one cannot help feeling at home. They are all old settlers around here and are well to do farmers in very comfortable pleasant homes. There is no sectarian or religious set here. There are some Spritiualists, but everyone is cultivated and refined and intelligent. I know you would like the society here. I am more in love with the country than I thought I could be with a strange one so soon, but everything seems just as it used to in Michigan in the Spring. The first flowers are blooming in the woods, the fruit trees are leafing out and everything seems like the old times.

All around our little house are lovely little groves and great mossy banks and a rippling little brook runs by us not far off. There are good farms for sale with buildings and orchards etc. around here for a reasonable sum. I am anxious you come. Remember you will not leave Frankie there, His presence will be with you here as much as there and there will not be so many painful associations here to bring to you mind your great loss. Try to think more of your future with him, and do not dwell too much on the past. My children are well and I try to realize what a blessing it is to be able to say that. I have been having my flower garden made. Thanks to my kind friends here I shall have over fifty varieties of flowers this summer. It will soon be time for strawberries; there are many wild ones. I wish you could come in time to enjoy the summer with us.

If you should come right away I will say this much by way of advice; do not take the emigrant train if you can avoid it; Do not take the cheapest hotels if you can avoid it; there are good accommodations to be had for $2.00 per day but not for $1.00. We were obliged to take the cheapest hotels but we run the risk of taking diseases of all kinds and had very poor fare. I only tell you this to let you know what to expect. I feel as if you was soon here, and hope it so. I want you where I can comfort and help you all in my power. Our bundle of bedding has not come yet. I begin to fear it has been lost, but it may come all right. When you come, try to secure a good map of the Pacific Coast so you can see just where you are going. Ed thinks this country will suit Isaac but it is not Paradise. It is much nearer it than Colorado ever will be.

May

Wooded Shore of the Willamette River Photo by June Morse

May's letter to Mother, April 17, 1876 - Spring Planting

Butteville Marion Co., Oregon,
Monday April 17, 1876

My Dear Mother-

Your very welcome letter came safely to hand a few days since and while baby Jessie is taking her afternoon nap and the boys are out in the woods with their father I will improve the time by writing to you. Your letter found us all well and busy doing the work that has to be done every spring by farmers and farmers' wives whether in Indiana or Oregon. The season has been so unusually wet here that farmers have not been able to plow very much yet and there will not be as large a crop put in as usual on that account. Everyone says there has not been such a wet winter for fifteen years as the last one was. The river is quite high and rising all the time. The weather is quite warm and when the sun shines you can almost see things grow. Our garden is coming on nicely. Since I wrote to you before we have bought us a little farm. It is such a small piece of land that it can hardly be called a farm, but it is large enough to make us a nice little home and on it we can raise all the fruit we can use and vegetables too. It is on the river and shall build our house where we can watch the steam boats pass up and down many times each day. It is only a quarter of a mile from where we live now and we intend to live here until our time is out (we rented for two years) and in the meantime put all of our spare time and means in improving our own little place. We want to get our trees set out this year and all kinds of fruit started and next year we will build. We have moved around so much that it is a great pleasure to both of us to feel that we can settle down and have a pleasant home to raise our children in and it is our intention to stay here a long as we live. As our means will enable us to, we can buy more land to raise grain and hay but for a few years we will have to rent. You said in your letter that Frank intended to come out here if we stay. I would be very glad to have him come and think there is no better country for a young man to get a start. It is hard for me to realize that he is almost a man for I can remember so well when he was a baby. But time flies and in a few weeks more I shall arrive at my twenty-sixth birthday. My Freddie is a great stout, hearty five-year-old, Eddie is past three and Jessie is fifteen months old and just commenced running alone. You have never said in your letters what business or trade Frank intends to follow. There would be a good chance here for a school teacher if he is fitted for that. There is plenty of work of all kinds and wages are very fair. If he should come, I would advise him not to stop in Colorado. It will cost a great deal more and I am positive that he would never be satisfied to stay there. He can get a ticket from Chicago to San Francisco as cheap as from Chicago to Denver. Alice and her family will be here as soon as they can sell their property there. Poor sister Alice—what a hard time she has always seen. It seems as though she has more trouble than one person can bear. She takes the death of little Frankie with more resignation than I ever thought she could, he was the idol of her heart and I know she must be lonely without him. My heart aches for her in her sorrow. No one knows all her mistakes and follies in life so well as I do, yet I pity her so much because she has suffered so much. I hope they will come and get a home near us and that we shall be able to spend the remainder of our lives near each other. I fear Rensselaer is so estranged from us we shall never meet him again. I shall be very glad to have Frank come here if he can and we will help him with our influence and friendship all we can. We are poor and cannot offer pecuniary aid to him and I know as long as he keeps his heath he will be able to take care of himself. I shall be proud to have such a brother and am glad he has stayed at home and acquired steady and useful habits. Your children are scattering, dear, Ma, as I suppose mine will do some day. But I am trying as you have done all your life, to do a mother's duty and if I fail it will be through ignorance. I shall ever bear a loving remembrance of you and tell my little ones about you so they may learn to love you, even if they never see you. Please write when you can. It does me good to get your letters; tell Frank to write too. Give my love to the rest of the home folks. Do you see Nettie very often—give her my warmest love.

Mary

May's letter to Alice, May 10, 1876 - Sympathy

Wednesday Morning,
May 10th, 1876

My darling sister.

Your letter dated April 23rd came to me late night and while the children are eating their breakfast I will add a few more to the letter already written. I wish it was in my power to say something to comfort you in your deep affliction, but I know that to you all words would sound hollow and unmeaning. Nothing but time will heal a broken heart; but my dear sister I wish you would try to look away from the darkest side and think of him as in a bright happy world waiting for you. He is not in the grave, but in a new form he is enjoying the bliss of that life that we will all know some day. I cannot make the children realize or understand that Frankie is dead. I do not want to cloud their minds with a fear of death, but I teach them that he is gone from this world to a better one where he will never suffer or cry anymore, and that some time we are all going to him. But I know that to you, surrounded as you are by all the things that are associated with his memory, it is harder to bear the loss. But take comfort in that sweet promise that he so continually lisped to you while living "Mama, I love you and I will never leave you." I think the angels must have put that in his little heart to try to impress it on you. He loves you still and will never leave you. Even though you may have many years to live here, that blessed presence will never leave you. To me it seems a beautiful thought that you have a guidance by that little hand beyond the veil. This thought and belief is as much a part of my life as my earthly loves are. I could not live without the blessed hope of the life to come. And tho it is so hard to give up our little ones, it would be worse to be called away and leave them alone motherless. For the sake of your baby and husband try to be more cheerful. Do not cloud that little baby heart too much with your sorrow. You have a work to do in molding his character and training him to a useful happy life. Be to him a mother in every sense, even if the most tender part of your love was given to Frankie do not let that fact keep all other loves out. But it is of no use for me to say this, for you have a mother heart as well as I, and that will not allow you to miss your duty. This is the day that the great Centennial Fair begins; but in our little world everything is as quiet as usual. We are having lovely weather now, and nature puts on a more beautiful aspect every day. I wish I could send you a bouquet of lilac and myrtle blossoms that is on my stand, it is so sweet.....

MOVE TO CABIN HOME IN BUTTEVILLE

It was a beautiful June day and Ed had finished the house on the three acre property that he had bought from Mr. Graham. Since the rental contract had been agreed to be over as soon as they moved into their new house, and the growing of the hops was ended in April, Ed had more time to clear some of his land and build their own house.

May was busy packing and their new house was so close that they ended up just piling things in the wagon to take over and then coming back for another load. She was glad to finally go to her own house. Ed would also build a barn and a root cellar to store the winter vegetables. They had already had a chance to put in some fruit trees and strawberries.

May was thinking how far they had come and how it had worked out to have their own place. She was interrupted by Freddie and Eddie asking if they could ride the wagon to help unload.

"Next time boys," she told them. "First help put my books in the trunk."

"Okay Mother," answered Freddie. He and Eddie enjoyed looking through the books that hid so many wonderful stories.

May carefully laid the pictures she had of her family back in Indiana on top wrapped in her best skirt. On the next load Ed hauled out the trunk and the bedding, the stove and the pots and pans. They all went to help unload. After the bedding was dumped on the bed, May put Jessie down in the middle for a nap. She busily put things away the best she could. It was a small house with their bedroom downstairs. The kitchen was in back too leaving the front room a parlor and space for a table next to the kitchen.

She was glad Ed was handy at carpentry. Even though the furniture was rough hewn it was sturdy. He had built shelves in the kitchen and a closet hutch in the bedroom. There was a narrow stairway at the end on the house that led to the boy's loft bedroom. Jessie still slept near her in a small crib.

"Where would you like the trunk?" called out Ed as he staggered through the doorway. He put it down while May gave him an answer. She wanted to keep a close eye on the family pictures.

"In the bedroom please, and Jessie's sleeping on our bed so do stay as quiet as you can."

He managed to shove the trunk across the floor to the bedroom. May caught him and stopped him with a hug. She knew how hard he had worked to make this possible.

"We'll try the new bed later," he looked at Jessie sleeping in the bedding, and smiled at May. She smiled too and went on with her work.

The boys came in with some lettuce they picked for supper and May started organizing the kitchen. Ed went outside to finish the privy shed making one of the seats lower for the children. The boys ran back out to overview the work and then started digging in the loose dirt piles.

May was thrilled to set up housekeeping in their own place. As the days went by she and Ed were very close and occasionally had some time in the evening to look out at the river and talk after the children were in bed.

"I'd like to get some more land to grow wheat and grain," Ed disclosed.

"It will be nice when Alice and Isaac get here and he can work with you," She added.

"If he brings his teams, that will definitely help out. But I need to pay for this land before I go off and get more into debt." Ed sighed, "This job at the packaging plant doesn't pay much and I know I could do well with grain without any grasshoppers."

"That's true, and we'll have one more mouth to feed next year." May let Ed know her present state.

Ed leaned over and gave her a little kiss, "I have fertile soil right next to me; growing babies is our best crop."

May beamed. Ed always knew what to say to make her feel happy. She snuggled to him as they made their way back to the house.

The Willamette River Photo by June Morse

MAY'S LETTER TO ALICE, JULY 16, 1876-LIFE BY THE WILLAMETTE

Butteville, Marion Co., Oregon,
At Home, Sunday, July 16, 1876.

Ever dear sister—

I had waited for seven weeks with all the patience I had for a letter from you and in all that time had received only a very short note (with the $15 order from Ira enclosed) but last Wednesday my reward came in receiving your nice long letter. It did me ever so much good, more than you can imagine, for I sometimes get very homesick and lonely, more than I ever did in my life before. To be sure we have plenty of neighbors who are pleasant and kind when I see them but sometimes the sense of loneliness comes over me so strong as to be almost unbearable, when I think of how far I am from you and the scenes and companions of former days. It is hard for me to think that I shall never be able to go back or see any of my loved friends. A long, long stretch of many hundred miles lies between us and I have not yet acquired any attachment for our new home and surroundings, although I suppose after a while I shall. I hope so for it has been so unpleasant to be longing all the time for something we can't have. We have been living in our place three weeks and are gradually getting things cleared up around us. I enjoy the location here very much. It is always cool on the river and we are not troubled with high winds or it is never sultry, there are no flies or mosquitoes so far. It is a very fine season, just rain enough.

There is considerable cloudy weather which is more pleasant than too much sunshine. Harvest is just commencing and bids fair to be a heavy one of wheat and oats. Our garden is in a splendid growing condition although pretty late on account of getting it put in late. I thought I had written you why Ed gave up the farm he rented. The main crop on it this year was hops and he soon found that it would take one man's time to tend them and there was so much other work to do that he would have to hire a man all the time. Hops are a very uncertain crop to market, sometimes they are as high as $.35 per lb., last year they were only $.12 and dull at that. Unless they bring in a high price there is no money in them and as there is a big crop raised this year they will be a low price. Ed saw that with the hired man and low price for hops he would not make a cent this year and so they threw up the contract and he got $25 a month from the time we came here till he quit, just three months. Everyone around here thinks he did well to get out of it so well as Mr. Graham has the name of being a hard man to deal with, penurious and sometimes unscrupulous. By doing as he did, we have got on our own place much sooner than we otherwise could, where we can raise our own living every year and he can have most of the time to work out. He gets $1.50 per day and boards at home and has time evenings for working in the garden considerable. After we get our little place all put in and producing something we can make a good living on it and some to spare without working so very hard as those who keep big farms. I am so anxious for you to have a place near us so the men can help each other and where you and I can be near enough to see each other every day. Be just as saving as you possibly can of your money so that when you come you can buy a place all cleared and improved and with fruit bearing orchards. There are such places to be had quite reasonably and then you could have a good living from the first and not work so hard, I am glad this is such a good year in Colorado and if every year was as good it would do you to stay there. But there has never been a failure here of fruit or grain nor is there likely to be. You must make up your mind to endure the rainy winters and it is not half as bad as you imagine. The rain falls so soft and slow that it does not make the walking very bad and there are very few days in their ordinary winter when a person with overshoes and waterproof cannot go where they please. And with plenty to eat in the cellar, good wood to blaze in the fireplace and a cozy home circle, one can put in a very pleasant winter.

The spring, summer and fall is delightful. From the time that strawberries come, generally about the middle of May, there is a constant succession of fresh fruit until winter sets in. We cannot take pleasure trips to the mountains as you do, but for 50 cents you can get on a boat and go anywhere from Portland to Salem and see beautiful scenery all the way. Then the woods here are so beautiful this summer to walk in. I long for your company to be with me on my frequent rambles around here. I think it would be a very sensible idea for you to come through with your teams for you would save so much money. It would not do to start before the first of May. Our nearest neighbors, Mr. Zoomalts, came here thirty years ago with ox teams from Missouri. They were six months on the road. It is much safer and pleasanter now and shorter and better roads have been made. Our Fourth was a very quiet one at home, not even a fire cracker here. They had big times in Portland, the boats were crowded with passengers. I thought of you all day and wondered if you was having a nice time. Your home must be beautiful this summer. I wish you could bring it out here. We received the $10 order from Isaac and the $30 and $15 from Ira. I mentioned it before, but perhaps you did not get the letter. I think it is a blessing for you to have that little girl, and still more so for her. You may be the means of making a noble woman of her, and she will be such a comfort to you.

MAY'S LETTER TO ALICE, AUGUST 6, 1876 - SPIRITUALISTS

Butteville, Marion Co., Oregon, at Home,
Sunday, August 6ᵗʰ, 1876.

Ever dear sister—

I received on Thursday last your letter which was mailed from Boulder, July 26 and came through in eight days, the quickest time that one has made it yet. This warm weather finds us all usually well though of course any one feels rather weak in such weather. It has not rained here for four weeks but things are not dried up as much as one would suppose. There is considerable cloudy, cool weather and very heavy dews at night so rain is not so much needed. They say it never rains here during harvest. Fall wheat as all cut and a splendid crop is reported. Spring grain is not ripe yet. When they harvest here on the prairie where for miles there is nothing but waving fields of grain, they use a header which keeps four or five wagons busy carrying the heads to the thrasher which runs with it; thus you see they make quick work of harvesting. On this side of the river, where it is all cleared land that is farmed, it is too hilly and stumpy to use the headers. I have never been around to see the country yet but this fall we are going down to Portland with a team and can see considerable in that way. I was up to Butteville last week for the first time since last May. I went up Monday evening and came back Tuesday evening. I always enjoy a visit with dear little Mrs. Galland and feel at home when there. I believe I have told you before that Spiritualism is a strong power in this community They hold camp meetings all the time at some point and seem to have big times. Last week and the week before, they held one near Butteville and when I was up there I was calling on a lady who had called on me and I got some acquainted with the Lecturess and great Spiritualist doctress. Mrs. Patterson (formerly her name was Dr. Finch) She had just come to Oregon and has been for years traveling all over the United States lecturing and practicing medicine. She doctors all manner of diseases and says it is through the influence of an Indian doctor. She certainly performs wonderful cures through some agency. I was not very favorably impressed with her, but her followers worship her. She is a clairvoyant medium. Our nearest neighbors (Mr. Zoomalts, who live on a hill just across our garden) are strong spiritualists and Mrs. Zoomalt and some of her daughters are mediums. I promised to attend one of their circles some time to see if I could get any satisfaction. I am willing to try anything or make any sacrifice to become convinced beyond the shadow of a doubt that those who have passed away are still living and can let us know it. It would be a great comfort to me if I could know that the spirits of those I love are hovering about me and caring for me. If there is such a thing possible I mean to get a test that will settle my mind. And yet I have not much faith in medium spiritualism and fear I shall never be satisfied with anything in this world. But there have been in my life two or three instances when I felt that our mother was near and telling me what to say and do. I know that twice, anyway, I have been drawn from the greatest danger through some supernatural agency. You know that I mean at Cold Water and at Net Fields. No one but you shares this secret with me about the letter. Of course Ed is opposed to spiritualism but still my happiness depends to a great extent on my own mind and if I can become satisfied on these points I am going to do it. Professor Baldwin (who I see was in Boulder City in May) has been in Portland last week. His lectures and performances were attended largely. It will be a grand thing when spiritualism can be divested of these humbugs in the shape of manifestations and stand in its better lights. I have no faith whatever in wrappings, tippings, untying of knots, etc. but still I feel that the true essence of it is pure and good and not to be treated as a humbug. But wait till you come and we will try and see if we can do anything. You must have had a dreadful time going to Eli's. I would not want to live where I could not get away without breaking my neck, or pretty near it. I had some ripe pears and plums up to Butteville and some harvest apples. Ed brought me a few plums from Mrs. Gouldings the other day which were the finest I ever ate. They are called the peach-plum, and are plum grafts on a peach root; they grow as large as a peach and taste of both, they are simply delirious. Never mind, we'll have all these things in time, won't we? We have had some of the largest black berries I ever saw, large, sweet and juicy. We have all the green apples we want to use now, they make good pies and sauce. I have not put up any fruit yet and fear I can't, we have so much to do this year. I don't feel able to buy the cans, jars, etc. but next year I will. We have a real good garden which gives us a good living now and mean to buy a cow this fall. We buy a quart of milk a day and go without butter most of the time; but it won't make any difference next year that we eat this year. I only hope and pray that you can sell there and come here in a year or less. I know you or Isaac will never regret it after you once get here. I am so sorry you had to give up your little girl. You will have to do as I did, get one of your own. But wait till you come to Oregon and I'll tell you how. Kiss dear little Lawrence, I know he must be real sweet now. Tell Media that I have waited for a letter from her till my patience is well nigh gone. I guess her love for me could never have been very great or she would not so soon forget me.. I am looking anxiously for your photographs, don't forget them. ...

MAY'S LETTER TO ALICE, NOV. 12, 1876 - GARDEN HARVEST

At home, Sunday evening.
Nov. 12 1876

My dearest sister—

Your letters of Oct 16nd. and Also of Oct 27— are both unanswered before me and as the little ones are all asleep and Ed is dividing his time between the last Christian Union and a plate of apples, I will try to write. Our mail comes in Mrs. Gouldings box at Butteville and she has learned to know your handwriting and knows how anxious I always feel to get your letters, so as soon as she sees a letter from you when her mail is brought she runs to her kitchen door and hangs out a white flag, which, as soon as I see, causes me to drop everything and run up there for your precious letters. Mrs. Goulding and her dear old mother, who lives with her, are such good neighbors and have kindly interested themselves in me and mine so that it is so pleasant for me to go there. I like all of our neighbors but theirs is the most pleasant place to go to. Well the middle of November finds us still busy and lots to do. The weather continues good and very large crops are being put in all over the state. We just finished digging our potatoes yesterday and Ed has worked all day today putting away the last of them in the cellars. He made a cellar on the bank of the river so when he wants to sell he will not have to haul them. He had 300 bushels in all and have over two hundred to sell. Some of them were injured by being too wet and some are too small to sell, but we sorted them as we picked them and have 240 bushels of nice large ones. We think that is a fair crop off from our little garden spot which contains only an acre and a half all together and raised besides the potatoes 400 head of cabbages, 25 bushels of carrots besides lots of beans, beets, turnips, onions & c., Potatoes are selling now at 40-50 cts. Per bu. but everyone predicts high prices before spring. Ed will keep his till spring. We have some of the largest ones and nicest ones I ever saw. Freddie and I picked up and sacked while Ed dug and it was fun to help when they were so nice. This week we are going to put out a big strawberry bed and transplant grapes, raspberry bushes, currants and other kinds of small fruit—so to have them growing. We already have out over a hundred currant bushes some of which will bear some next year. It seems so nice to be putting out such things and planning to make us a home for life surrounded by these luxuries and necessities. I never felt so satisfied and hopeful about any other place we ever had. You remember last spring I wrote you about a piece of land for sale joining ours, and afterwards told you it was sold. We learned a few days ago that it was not sold and is still for sale. It does not quite join us as I thought, but is only a very little way down the river from us, less than ¼ of a mile. It contains 40 acres of good farming land, a little of it is cleared, and plenty of cord wood can be cut on it to pay for it. Enough of it lays on the river for a nice home to be built up and Ed thinks it is a very desirable place and plenty large enough for one man to manage. He hopes Isaac will like it well enough to take it and then we will be neighbors all our lives, which is to me a

happy thought. Perhaps you will not like it. (the place
I mean) but you can at least come and see yourselves.

We have not learned yet who is elected President..
Oregon went 1400 majority Republican–every other
year since it was a State it has been Democratic. I see
Colorado went Republican strong. Good for her.

Please don't wait if I am not prompt about writing. I
write just as often as I feel as if I had anything of
interest to write and am very busy most if the time. I
hope to get a letter from you soon.

NOTE: *Rutherford B. Hays was elected president after a bitterly disputed
election to office by one electoral vote.*

1877
ED'S PERSPECTIVE

ED LYMAN'S LETTER TO ISAAC JAN.7, 1877

Butteville, Marion Co., Oregon
Jan. 7ᵗʰ, 1877.

Friend Issac;

We received yours last evening and I take the first oper'
to answer it. We are very glad to hear from you. You are
having snappy cold weather you say and dogs and all of
that. The weather here is quite a contrast. Last month we
had it cold enough to form a thin scale of ice on the wash
dish, it froze the ground an inch deep in open ground but

thawed out every day. It did not freeze potatoes that were in the ground. We had about a week or so of such weather. Now we are having spring weather. You will see a fly buzzing around every once in a while, grass is growing, frogs are croaking, sort of soft rain falls once in a while. It is delightful weather, we have had no snow nor ice on the river so far although we expect a little cold weather next month. You ask me how much land I have. Quite a small piece, only three 3 acres. It is a very rich piece of land. I am going into gardening and small fruits such as strawberries, currants, raspberries, blackberries, grapes, peaches, peach-plums, prunes and some few apples. I want to set out my fruit next spring. I have some set out already. I want more land when I am able to pay for it but I can make a good living on this by working out what spare time I have after my fruit comes on. Then I will be all right. You speak of sending me money. I hope you will, because I have to pay for my land in March, $200 dollars. I am paying 12 percent annum interest which is more than I am getting from you. I have not paid any on the land yet. When I got here and bought me a few dishes and stove I had 60 cents left for seed. I have had to work to a disadvantage all the time. I have had to work by day to get a living for me and mine and walk a mile and a half part of the time night and morning to my work. I got from a dollar to a dollar and a half a day in harvest, $1.50 are the wages. In the mean time I have raised my own vegetables for the year, built a house and a small barn myself, dug a cellar under my house and another for vegetables outside and cleared up about an acre and a half of my land and set out considerable small fruit and bought me a cow and numerous other things and we are pretty well clothed for the season and I balance my account today and what do I find. I find I have a cow 150 lbs. Pork 40 lbs. beef, two pigs, 250 bushel of potatoes, beans and other vegetables to do us. 20 bushels apples, and a wife and three children that are well and able to eat their rations and I am not in debt for anything but the land. How has this been brought about! By hard work, economy, and paying as you go, run up no store bills, sit on stools, make a table and bedstead out of rough lumber and my wife and I talk over our prospects together and work together to our own advantage, wear patched pants and have one or two calico gowns and everything else in proportion, but always enough to eat. I thought we were pretty saving in Colorado but comparing the two, we were quite extravagant in Colorado I thought I had worked hard in Colorado but I have worked harder here. I have had no team to work with, only as I hired, instead of a team I have used bone and muscle. I have had one year's experience here and next year will not be as hard on me if I get my land paid for. When you send money, send money order drawn on Portland, Oregon.

(this from Ed Lyman)

MAY'S BABY FRANK

With Springtime coming on it was time to plant the garden. Ed helped May since it was almost time to have their next child and she could hardly lean over. Freddie helped cover the seeds. He was a good worker for a six year old. Ed and May had been to Portland in the fall to find a doctor. He recommended a mid-wife Mrs. Kirkley in South Portland, since there weren't any in Butteville area. May had visited her a few times to remind herself to care of her health and not repeat the last pre-delivery sickness she had with Jessie. She felt fortunate that the baby was due in the spring instead of the middle of the winter.

One morning May felt the pains coming. Ed fed the children and they were off on the steamboat to Mrs. Kirkley's. The children were excited about going through the locks at Willamette Falls across from Oregon City which allowed passage to Portland. They liked to watch the water lower the steamboat to the next level. This was one time May could've done without the delay. Shortly they were at South Portland within walking distance to the Kirkley's.

Carry Kirkley was from Sweden and had two children, Maggie – 5 who took after her with beautiful flaxen hair, and Billy – 3 who had dark hair like his father. There was another child on the way in a few months. She welcomed them in and Eddie and Jessie stayed there to play with the other children, while Fred went with Ed to Portland on errands. Sure enough by the time they got back May was working hard to give birth and a few hours later a fine boy was born. Ed took the children home to give May some time to rest with their new baby.

After a few days he returned to accompany her home with their still un-named boy. Later named him Franklin Raymond born March 20, 1877.

Steamboat "Gov. Grover" in Willamette Falls Locks - 1873
This early view shows both the locks and the steamboat Governor Grover the year they were completed. She was not long-lived, being dismantled in Portland in 1880.-- This photo is restored and printed by *Old Oregon*. Original courtesy of the Clackamas County Historical Society.
Photo is from oldoregonphotos.com

MAY'S LETTER TO ALICE, APRIL 6, 1877- MAY'S FRANK

Friday Afternoon
April 6, 1877

Just as we were at dinner a neighbor brought your letter of March 22nd containing the P.O. Order and a package of papers for all of which we are thankful to you. But I was disappointed in not receiving a nice long letter from you, for it has been some time since I had one. But it encourages me so much to think that the time will soon come when we can say what we cannot write to each other. I hope the spring there is as forward as it is here, so you can start early. Everything bids fair to produce large crops this year and the weather is perfect just rain enough and none too much. I am gaining strength slowly but surely and shall soon be a well as ever. Baby grins finely and is so good. We have about decided to call him Frank Raymond. Ed seems anxious to call him Frank and I added the other name. It will come a little hard for me to become accustomed to call him by the name that has so many tender memories connected with it, but perhaps it will keep me more loving and gentle and patient. He is a sweet little fellow and I know you will have a warm spot in your heart for my Frankie as I always had for yours. If you visit Media before you leave give her and Ira our best wishes and tell them for me they will find a welcome here if they ever see fit to visit Oregon. Media gave me a bound volume of Today's Lady's Book and I forgot it and left it at your house I was sorry. For I feared she would think I did it purpose, but I really would have liked it, and if you have it I hope you will bring it. Ed was very glad to get the money as the note was due yesterday. He can't pay more than half of it this year but we hope to make something on the place this year. There has been no market for potatoes this winter and he has not sold many. The drought in California this year will make better market here...

ALICE'S LETTER TO MOTHER, APRIL 15, 1877- OFF TO OREGON

Red Hill, Colorado,
April 15, 1877

My dear Ma and All-

Today being quite long and somewhat lonesome, I will try to pass a little time away in writing home, Although it seems to me it don't do much good for my letters home are never, or seldom, answered and I don't get much encouragement from writing, but we are soon to leave our mountain home for the more genial climate of Oregon, and as our long journey of 16 hundred miles with teams may be endangered by Indians, and many other things, we may possibly never see our Oregon home, and such things being possible I will write once more here, and after we get through, if we do. We will start in three weeks or less and expect to be about two months and a half on our way, going to Salt Lake City, will stop two or three days there, then go north to Boise City, Idaho Territory, then west to the Pacific Coast. In going this way we avoid the worst part of the

Indian country, and perhaps get through all right. We are anxious to be off or more so to get there, and be building up a home as we have failed to do in this grasshopper country. I almost regret to leave our little Mountain Nest as it is such a lovely spot and if my husband's health was better we could do very well here with our stock, but if it were not for the "hoppers" we could raise everything to perfection, but as it is we can't depend on anything. Only think, last spring Isaac put in 35 acres of corn, which promised as well as ever a crop did anywhere and just before it began to ripen, down came the grasshoppers in a cloud and in less than two days there was nothing left but a short bare stalk, Just so with everything else, except wheat last year which was being harvested when they came so when winter came we had every bite our horses and stock ate, to buy and everything we ate, but flour, so how is a farmer to get ahead any, at this rate. We have 13 cows which provide butter and milk, plenty, but dairy business is out of our line. Isaac hates to milk and I hate to make butter so we rent out our cows on shares. We have 8 head of horses, but our range being excellent we let them all run at large but from 2 to 4 work horses, If it were not for the hoppers this would be one of the best countries in the world, but they are here so bad, coming every fall, and laying the whole country full of eggs, then hatching out in the spring. Many think they always will be here. Well, perhaps grasshoppers don't interest you as much as you never saw them, so I will, drop a few family notes and close. We are all pretty well now, Isaac is taking his Sunday lunch, little Lawrence is asleep in his cradle, and he looks awful sweet too. He grows to look more like Frankie every day, only he has spunk while Frankie was very quiet disposition, but he is a spoiled pet, all the baby I've got. Sister May has another boy, born on the 20th of March last. I have heard from her twice since, she is getting along nicely, she has four children now, three boys and a sweet little queen Jessie. Oh I am so anxious to get settled near her and help her with her much care. Ed is doing first rate in Oregon but he is one of that kind of men, that is bound to do well. He is so ambitious that nothing stops him. He is one of the best of husbands to May so she is always well cared for. Now Ma, I want some of you to write immediately, so that I can hear from home once more. We are going with two teams and will sell our cattle and take the rest of the horses with us. We start with a company, mostly neighbors and relatives, so don't worry about us. I forgot to tell you that cousin Media and her mother, my aunt, Uncle Isaac Olny's wife from Lawrence, Kansas made us a visit two weeks ago. Media married in this country a year ago, has a nice boy now. Aunt Delia has now gone home. Give our love to Nettie and Dora and tell them to write, but don't any of you direct your letters to Colorado after the 6th of May, but until then direct the same as before, Pella P.O., Bolder Colorado, after that to Butteville, Marion Co. Oregon.

(This from Alice)

MAY'S LETTER TO FRANK, AUGUST 27, 1877- CHINESE LABOR

Butteville, Marion Co., Oregon, Monday evening,
August 27, 1877.

Dear brother Frank.

Your very welcome letter was received two weeks ago and I meant to have answered it sooner but every day my time is so fully occupied by my work that I find no time to write unless I do it after all the little ones are in bed, as I am doing now. You may well imagine that with four little ones to look after and all my work to do, I have not much time to play, so you will please excuse me for being so negligent about writing. I think of you all very often and wish I could hear from you more often. I wonder if I shall ever be permitted to see any of the dear familiar faces that surrounded my earliest childhood years. I fear not, for Oregon is a long ways from Indiana and poor folks have no money to spend in making visits, so unless you come west I am afraid I shall never see you. I am looking for Alice now all the time. They have been nearly three months on the road and I think they will be here this week or next. I have heard from them three or four times since they started and from their letters I judge that they have had a hard trip. It is a long trip and a hard one but a man saves money by coming with his teams. We shall always wish we had come with our team. We like Oregon very much indeed and I do not think we could be induced to leave it for any other country in the U.S. The climate is so mild in the winter, and though some people complain of too much rain, I think it is preferable to snow and cold. Last winter we did not see snow enough to half cover the ground, nor freezing weather enough to make ice in the house any night. The summers are cool enough to suit anyone; the nights are always cool and there are no mosquitoes to sing you to sleep either. Every kind of grain, fruit and vegetable grows here and produce enormous crops and bring fair price in the market. Our home is right on the Willamette river and nearly any time in the day we can see a steamboat passing up or down. It makes it very pleasant and also very convenient for when a man has any produce to sell he can take it to the bank and wave his hat and the boats will take it for him. We are only 18 miles from Portland and about the same distance from Salem, the capital. The Willamette Valley is very thickly settled and has been for years, but there are other vallies in different parts of the state said to be just as good as this when they are developed. I do not know where Alice and her husband will want to go. I hope they will find a home near us for it would be so pleasant for me to have them within visiting distance. I am glad to know that Rensselaer is doing well and hope he will marry a good woman and settle down and be a good steady man. I have not seen him for twelve years and have not had a letter from him for six years. Mr. Johnson (the man I lived with four years after Pa died) who now lives in Hudson, Mich., wrote me last June that Rensselaer had just made him a short visit and seemed to be a pretty good young man......I suppose he has wandered about for so many years that it would require considerable resolution on his part to settle down. It is one of the worst things a young

man can do to form the habit of roaming about constantly.
I am glad you have refrained from doing so and hope you
never will. This is not a very good country for a young
man to come to for several reasons. First, the society here,
as a rule, is not good. There is a very large proportion of
the inhabitants that is made up of single men, young and
old, and of the roughest class. Intemperance has a strong
hold on most of the men and all the other vices follow in its
lead. I sincerely hope there will be a great change before my
boys grow up and think there will be as eastern people are
coming in all the time who are of the better class and will
probably in time make a better society. I am very thankful
to have a husband who never touched a drop of liquor or
used tobacco or uttered an oath in his life and we hope to
keep our children from the evil that surrounds us. Another
reason why this is not a good country for young men who
depend on their labor for a livelihood is the low wages that
laborers get. The country is full of Chinamen who can cook
for almost nothing and live like beasts and farmers will
hire them because they work cheap. A white man would
starve to death on a Chinaman's wages to say nothing of
trying to support a family. It is generally believed that
there will be a war on this coast on account of so many
Chinese coming in. They are sent here by hundreds on every
ship and are to be found in all branches of industry, thus
driving the white men and women to work for their wages or
not work at all. I do not know what can be done about it,
but something will have to be done. This is the finest fruit
country I have ever lived in, from the early spring we have
had a constant succession of beautiful fruit of every variety

and in abundance. We have also had an excellent garden. It will be three years before we shall have fruit of our own (except berries, which come on quickly) but there is plenty in the neighborhood and we have all we want. The children are all healthy and happy. Little Jessie, our only girl, is a wee mite of a creature but healthy. Baby Frank, now nearly six months old, is a fat, rosy little blue eyed fellow and a great pet with us all. The boys, Freddie and Eddie, are big strong boys able to do a good deal to save me steps and are a great comfort to me. I am not very stout this summer but manage to keep around and do my work which is light and easy generally. Well it is getting late and all the rest are in bed and asleep so I guess I had better stop writing for this time. As soon as Alice gets here, either she or I will write you at once. Please write often. Give my warmest love to Ma and Nettie and Dora and the rest. Tell Nettie to write to me and I will answer immediately. I have her picture and look at it often and wonder if she ever thinks of me. Well, good bye.

Your affectionate sister,

May G. Lyman

ALICE AND ISAAC ARRIVE IN OREGON

What a wonderful sight when Alice and Isaac arrived at May and Ed's farm in Butteville Oregon. The two teams pulling the covered wagon rattled through the field and May rushed out at the sound waving both arms. The long shadows of the trees in the late afternoon accentuated the contrast with the sunny fields. Isaac stopped the horses who snorted and glistened in the sun.

He secured them and then carefully helped Alice down from the wagon. She looked tired but cheerful and May ran to greet her giving her a hug with space for the baby belly.

"Oh Alice, how are you?" quizzed May. "Come in and rest, I'll put some tea on." May helped her in and settled her on the settee.

"I thought we'd never get here. It's so good to see you," moaned Alice. Isaac brought Lawrence in. Freddie and Eddie immediately started to entertain him. But it was Jessie who stole the show. The two year olds stared at each other, Jessie with her curly brown hair and Lawrence with his fair complexion. Jessie shyly offered to share her picture book and Lawrence awkwardly gave her a hug. Isaac excused himself and went out to tend the teams.

While Alice lay down to rest, May made some tea and got Frank out of the crib from his nap.

"Thank you May, for having some idea of what we went through, but it was so long going through the mountains then the endless plains and more mountains." Alice smiled.

"How wonderful for you to finally get here." exclaimed May.

She served the tea to Alice who by this time was sitting up watching little Frank trying to crawl.

"I've been waiting for you dearest sister, I am so happy you are here safely with no harm to you or your family." May handed some apple pieces to the children. "How good Lawrence looks."

"He did very well, but was confined during travel when all he wanted to do was run around." Alice sipped her tea and had some apple. "This apple is so good I think that I could live on fruit from the lack of them."

"Here, have some strawberry jam made from our own strawberries." May spread some jam on a biscuit and gave it to Alice.

"This is heavenly! I'm already feeling better about coming. It was very hard to sell everything and pack only what we needed." Alice sighed.

"How is Media and Ira?" asked May.

"She has a sweet son, a big baby. Her mother couldn't wait to come visit to see her grandson. Aunt Delia and Edwin Waugh are very good for each other. They still have Willie to bring up, but he's doing well in school and works delivering newspapers after school." Alice explained as she lay back down.

The children had gone outside showing the garden and their favorite places to play to Lawrence. Isaac came in and had some tea and biscuits with jam. He had washed up outside by the pump and surveyed all Ed's improvements.

"Looks like Ed's been planting some trees," he observed.

"Yes we hope to grow some of those peach-plums that I told you about, Strawberries are a sure pick," May added. "We go into Portland and get a good price for any produce we grow."

"Well, Alice and I will have to find a place nearby and have a little farm too." He handed Alice a cloth to wipe off some spilled jam. she sat back up and wiped her dress.

"May, we'll be close again, sharing our families. Please come and be with me for this next one." Alice looked at May's shining eyes. "It won't be long now, the end of October."

"I promise to be there; I'll come early and we'll have lots of time to visit," planned May.

"Howdy folks," as Ed appeared at the door. "Mighty nice teams you have Isaac." He crossed the room and they had a hearty hand-shake and clap on the back.

"You're looking fit," observed Isaac.

"There's the one looking fit." Ed bent over Alice and gave her a kiss on the cheek.

"You managed to make it in one piece," he told her.

"You can say that now, Ed Lyman, just wait," Alice retorted. "I'm going to steal your wife for a while next month."

"She's already made up her mind," returned Ed. "How did the Chapmans make it," he inquired. He was concerned about Isaac's sister Maria.

"Uncle Eri, Maria and her family stopped at Hubbard. They knew someone there and it seems that Eri will be farming in the area." Isaac filled him in.

"It was very nice to have their help along the way," Alice continued. "The older three children were very good watching the younger three; and Lawrence at 2 years was the same age as Alma. Of course their baby Lulu was only one year so Maria had her hands full, besides being two months sick. I had a chance to help her with Lulu." Alice smiled thinking of her own baby.

They spent the evening catching up on the trip and sharing memories. The children were having a great time together and there was no mention of Alice's Frankie. The children all slept in the loft together and the women got the bed next to May's little Frank in the crib. The men took the wagon.

The next morning after a lingering breakfast, Alice and Isaac went to find a place to rent leaving Lawrence in May's care. When they returned they had found a place a few miles from May and closer to Butteville. They could easily walk into town for anything they might need.

ALICE'S BABY CORA

The time came for Alice to have the baby and true to her word May was there two weeks early just in case. The sisters had a lovely visit caring for the children and having time to remember Alice's little angel Frankie. Alice got to know Jessie and Frank. They had many a laugh over Lawrence doing whatever Jessie asked him to do, and Frank trying to keep up crawling.

On November 5th Little Cora was born. Alice had gone into labor late in the evening and by morning the baby arrived. Alice worked all night catching cat naps while May cheered her on. They were both exhausted when the children woke up. Alice went back to sleep as May kept up with the children. Isaac was happy for Alice to have a girl. They all looked in at the new baby sleeping in the cradle. May stayed for several more days until Alice could take over her duties. Isaac helped with the morning chaos and cleaned up after supper.

How happy May was for Alice. She related the visit to Ed who was equally pleased for Alice. Now that Alice was nearby, Ed could see how happy it made May.

MAY'S LETTER TO SISTER NETTIE, NOV. 18, 1877 - HOMESTEADING

Butteville, Marion Co. Oregon, Sunday evening,
Nov 18, 1877

My Dear Sister Nettie;

It has been over a month since I received your letter and I have promised myself many times that I would certainly not let another day go by without taking the time to write to you. But my time seems to be so fully occupied in doing my work that there is never one spare moment. But it is such a treat to get letters from friends that I ought to be more punctual in answering them. We are all pretty well this fall; my baby has been pretty sick an account of teething but is well now. I don't know whether Alice has written to you since she came here or not. They reached our house on the 19th of September, after being three months and a half on the road. Of course they were tired out and glad to get to a stopping place. They do not like the country as well as they expected to and I don't know whether they will stay or not. They rented a place about three miles from our house and half a mile from Butteville. They have rented it for a year. I went over to their place four weeks ago today and stayed with her three weeks, coming home last Sunday. I left Alice with a fine little daughter in her arms of which they are very proud. It was born on the 5th of November. Alice got along pretty well considering what a hard summer's work she had done. Their little boy, two and a half years old, a healthy stout little fellow but is not so sweet and lovable as their little Frankie was.

If they stay in Oregon they will probably go somewhere and take up a homestead, we talk of going together, our family and theirs, and take up a homestead. I hope Alice and I can live near each other the rest of our lives. I like Oregon and have no desire to leave this part of the world. This has been a pretty good year for crops of all kinds, although there was a considerable rain during harvest which injured the grain crop some. Our house is right on the bank of the Willamette river, where the boats are passing all the time, and it is a good deal of company for me to watch them. We have all kinds of fruit and vegetables in abundance, good neighbors and it is very healthy here. I would never advise anyone to come to Oregon if they are doing well where they are. It is best to "let well enough alone" but I am glad we came, and would not leave if I could. It seems a long way from our old home and friends in Michigan, and Indiana, but when the Northern Pacific R.R. Is completed, it will take less than a week to go there. You and Dora ought to be getting rich enough by this time to think of making us a visit. As for me, I have too many babies to talk of going anywhere. I will take care of them now and in a few years they will pay me by taking care of me. I often think of you all and would like to hear from you all more often. Frank writes to me quite often. He writes such good, sensible manly letters, it is a comfort to have one good steady brother. Poor Rensselaer, I fear he will never be as good a man as his father was. But I have hopes of him yet. It is getting late and I will close by sending much love and good wishes to you all and hoping to hear from you soon. I remain as ever, your sister Of course when I write to you, I mean it for Dora too.

Mary G Lyman

1878
MAY AND ED'S MOVE TO NEWBURG

All this time of living on their farm, Ed had used the path on the side of Mr. Graham's field to access his property. All of a sudden Mr. Graham didn't want him running over his field, that he didn't have a right of way. Ed couldn't believe that Mr. Graham would sell him property without a right of way and asked him to give him or sell him the little strip of path next to his land for a right of way. Mr. Graham refused to do that and forced Ed to sell him back the farm property with all the improvements.

Ed tried to explain this to May who was in tears.

"If he won't sell us a right of way, then there's nothing I can do. He can keep us from getting to our farm," explained Ed.

"I had hoped we could stay here," replied May wiping her tears and assessing the situation. "We could really use a bigger house now that we have four children. The orchard won't be producing for another three years." She paused thinking again. "It's such a nice spot overlooking the river and close to Alice. Ed, can't we stay here? Isn't there some solution?"

"I'm afraid he has us over a barrel, the shyster, I'll have to start looking for another place. He said we could stay until we found something else." Ed felt very unhappy to uproot May when she finally felt settled.

May tried to console herself. Here Ed had worked so hard, and she felt content with the small place. But it was true; they needed a bigger place, more land for crops, and the children were growing up and needed to be near a school.

They celebrated the Christmas holiday with Alice and Issac's family. May enjoyed the time spent with the children. Little Cora was so sweet, and Frank was pulling himself up getting ready to walk. The other children played games, sung Christmas songs with the adults joining in, and everyone gave little handmade items.

How bittersweet to have the families together knowing that they would be moving again. May thought of all the times they had moved before, and realized that what was important was being together no matter where they were. She and Alice commiserated together and promised to stay in touch by writing letters.

As the weeks went by, Ed found a place on the west side of the river near Newberg and rented it from Mr. Parrish. It was a big log cabin with three separate bedrooms upstairs. It had a bigger sitting room and more storage space. The wood range was great and even had an oven. May was pleased that it was close to the Evarts school house three miles through the woods by trail. They moved late February of 1878.

MAY'S LETTER TO ALICE, FEB. 28, 1878- NEWBURG

Wednesday evening,
February 28, 1878

Dear sister---

As Ed is going over to the old place tomorrow, I will improve the opportunity to drop you a line. We did not get over here till Sunday afternoon about three o'clock, stayed at Mr. Zoomalts all night. I have done a big washing and got pretty well settled in our new quarters. I like it pretty well and think in the summer it will be quite a nice place to stay. We are all real well now and hope you are the same. I guess it would take you a week get over the worry of our long visit. You must write once in a while and I can get ours mailed every Saturday. Ed has been planting early potatoes today. We hope to have a nice garden here. I am afraid you will feel insulted at this bundle of old clothes but I thought it might save you a little sewing and they are of no use to me. I wish I was able to send the dear little baby girl something nice. These books I would like to have sent to Mrs. Galland as soon as you can conveniently. I ought to have sent them sooner.

I shall look for a letter from you soon with love to all I remain as ever,

Sister May.

MAY'S LETTER TO ALICE, JUNE 7, 1878 - PLANS FOR THE 4TH

At home, Sunday evening,
June 7, 1878.

Dear Sister--

Having a few minutes leisure before supper time, I will drop you a line. I found Ed waiting for me at Abernathy's landing that day and was so glad I had not disappointed him. I found things all right at home but needing me somewhat. I felt very tired for a few days and did not try to do much, but managed to get ready and go to a picnic yesterday about three miles from here. It was

got up by the Good Templars and passed off first rate.
Had Speaking, singing, a basket dinner etc. Got home
pretty tired last night but got up again this morning and
went off to a Camp Meeting about four miles from here
up on the mountain. Have just got home. We had two
services and enjoyed it first rate- but is dreadful tiresome
riding over the hills so much. As Ed is going up for our
mail tomorrow I thought I would write a little tonight.
Ed says it will be impossible for us to go to Salem on
the Fourth for several reasons and since the hot weather
came I don't care much about going. It will be so dusty
and hot, I fear we should not have fun enough to pay for
the trouble. There is to be a celebration here, at the same
place where the picnic was yesterday, they expect to have
a good time, speaking etc. and I guess we will go there.
Now I don't want to spoil your Fourth in the least.
Go if you wish and enjoy it just the same and more too,
enough for both of us.

But if anything should happen that you give up going
to Salem, come over here the day before and go with us. I
like the people around here first rate. They are nearly all
Eastern people and real friendly. It would be pleasant if
Eli's folks should come too, for if you don't go to Salem
of course they won't. Now do just what you think you
would most enjoy. I shall not give up going to Portland
this fall, but don't care so very much about Salem. I
found your pin in my basket when I got home, will save
it. I hope you have your fill of strawberries and cream.
My raspberries will be ripe in a week I think. Write
occasionally, and let me know what you will do about the
Fourth. Sister May. Monday morning. Have just been

writing a note to Media. Don't suppose she will answer though.

Over the summer May was sewing some school clothes for the two oldest boys and tending a vegetable garden. She was feeling very far from Alice having to write letters. But as least her health was good and Ed was working at home. She was pregnant again and got tired easily.

On the first day of school Ed went with Freddie and Eddie to blaze a trail connecting the trail from the Holstons, their neighbors, to the school house. The Holstons had three older children and William the same age as Fred, and Effa, Jessie's age and a baby boy. May was home with Jessie and Frank, with the next one due in February. She was content to help the children with their school work and teach the younger ones the alphabet. They loved having stories read to them and either she or Ed would read a story at bedtime, although Ed liked to make up his own. Then she could hear the children howling with laughter instead of going to sleep.

1879
MAY'S BABY CHARLIE

May's Letter to Alice, Jan. 10, 1879- Baby Plans

Friday, Jan 10, 1879.

Dear sister Alice.

I suppose it is about time for me to write but I hardly know how to do it. I have been very poorly the last two weeks, owing partly to a severe cold which brought on neuralgia and catarrh so that I am not good for much but have been better since the weather moderated. The children are all ailing, worms I guess. Ed has all the work to do so he has no time to get sick. About your coming over, how are we to arrange? I want you very much if you can come. I am afraid Isaac will think it is asking too much for him to bring you to the river but on account of the weather, roads, etc. that seems to be the safest way. If it is as cold as it had been it would not be possible to cross the river with a team. So if you can come about Saturday, the 25th, Ed will be on this side with his team. If it should be raining or stormy so you could not come then, the first pleasant day after that time will do. I am quite sure I shall keep up till the 30th anyway. If it should be so you can not come at all, don't worry about me. I can get along some how. If you come, bring a bed tick if you can and a little bedding as I have a scant supply for cold weather. I will try to pay you for all the trouble I put you to and hope Isaac won't think hard of it. Accidents will happen you know. I have had no letters from anyone yet. I wish you would bring me something to read. I would like to borrow your tatting shuttle too. I guess that is all. Now use your own judgment about coming, don't make any great sacrifice to do so. With love to all.

I remain as ever, your sister, *May Lyman.*

In January May was planning to have Alice come to help her with the birth of her fifth child. The weather had been cold and she was getting over a bad cold. She remembered how sick she had been with Jessie and was being very careful to get enough rest and eat right. But she was concerned that Alice might not make it to help her. Mrs Kirkley was away visiting her sister so May was determined to be with Alice. It continued to be stormy and Isaac didn't want Alice to go.

The first of February there was a break in the weather and Ed took May, Jessie, and Frank to the landing at Newberg where they crossed on the steamboat to Butteville, Isaac picked them up on the other side. Since the older boys were in school, Ed would have time to work and be back home for them later in the day.

Alice and Isaac now had a nice place in town. May felt at home there. She was glad to be with Alice who could care for Jessie and Frank as she had her baby, there was not much time waiting. Charles Henry was born in Butteville under the watchful eye of Alice and a new doctor in town. Ed had come to see how things were going and after a few days rest May returned home. The boys met her with hugs while Jessie was hanging on to her skirt. Baby Charley was asleep in her arms and they got to peek at his little face and hands. Ed meanwhile scooped up Frank and zoomed him around the room until he giggled with glee. The whole family was laughing and celebrating the new arrival.

The new routine kept the family going through to the spring. Fred and Eddie went to school while May took care of her babies. Jessie was old enough to be very helpful. It would be another year before she could go to school. She was so good with baby Charlie keeping him happy in the cradle that May had borrowed back from Alice. Frank was still using the crib in Jessie's room.

Ed was working on a deal to buy 80 acres from Mr. Holston. He was loaning the down payment from Isaac. Ed agreed to pay Holston $400 over four years with interest. He spent the summer clearing 20 acres of young timber. After slashing it and clearing it up, he fenced it and put in a big crop.

May's letter to Alice, May 27, 1879 - Diseases

Newberg Yamhill Co. Oregon, Monday Eve
May 27, 1879

Dear Sister,

I guess it is about time for me to write to let you know that we are all alive yet, for it seems as though the fates have ordained that we shall not see each other very soon. I have not written sooner for I expected to have been with you this week and got up very early last Sunday morning and we started for your place; but when we got to the river we could not cross. The water had washed out the roads so that the ferryman said it would not be safe to try to get over. You may be sure I was very much disappointed for I had been looking forward to this visit so long I could hardly bear to give it up after once starting. And now a worse obstacle than the river seems to rise up and threaten to keep me tied at home for the summer. Everyone in the neighborhood has the whooping cough and my children have been exposed and will be almost sure to have it. I think the baby is commencing to take it now for he has a very bad cough and is feverish and sick. I shall have my hands full if they all have it at once. The measles are all about us, too, and I am afraid to stir out for fear of the children taking both diseases together which the doctor says, is very apt to prove fatal. I want to see you more than you can think, but do not want to give your little-ones the whooping cough, so what can we do? My own health is improving and I am now about as well as I ever am when nursing a baby. I have not done much sewing yet but guess I can get it done some time. The weather is so horrid most of the time we all feel about sick. Have you any garden or fruit yet? We have a few currants and plenty of gooseberries and the children have found a few small sour strawberries. Our garden looks well but will not be very early. Ed is working on his place. He has been culling and peeling house logs for our cabin and is getting some slashing done. He plowed for Mr Gooze, Kirkley, & Ingalls last spring and takes his pay in slashing. He will have about fourteen acres to burn and put in this fall. Our crop here looks well so far but the winter grain would look better without so much rain. I am having success so far with chickens. I have about 150 now and will have some large enough to sell by the 10th of June. It takes a good deal of work to tend them but I hope to make something by it. I am making butter to sell all the time but it is very cheap now; the last I sold for 20cts. Well it is late and everyone is asleep and I feel as though I would like to be so I will not write more now. I am anxious to get a letter from you to know how you are all doing and feeling. Tell little Concis I thought of him on his birthday all day but could not come to see him. Kiss the little ones for me. I want to see them ever so bad. I have heard nothing from Indiana yet. I

wrote to Frank about two weeks ago and if I don't hear from
him by next month I shall do something desperate. I think it
is so strange the way they act. Please write if you cannot come.
Baby Charlie grows so fast. He is a very large and heavy
but is as sweet and pretty as a rose. I have had him in short
clothes three weeks.

Your Sister May

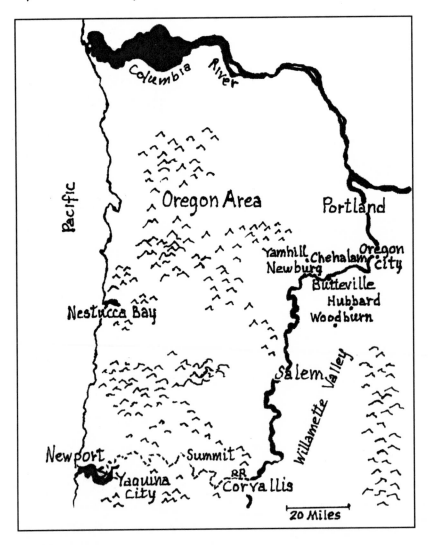

MAY'S LETTER TO ALICE OCT. 2, 1879- CROPS

Newberg, Yamhill Co., Oregon, Thursday eve,
Oct. 2ᵈ, 1879.

Dear Sister--

I am ashamed to think that I have waited a whole month since I saw you without writing and will try to scratch off a few words tonight although I am tired, having done a big washing today with a cross baby in the bargain. Well, I hardly know where to commence. We are all well as usual, though the children take turns having little sick spells that don't seem to amount to much but makes them cross. We got the last of our threshing done a week ago yesterday. There was only 150 bushels of the spring grain, 115 of wheat. Ed shipped 66 bushels last Friday. He got 95 cents for it at the landing. We went down to Portland Monday. Sept. 30. I took the children and had a tiresome time. It rained so we could not camp out and had to stop at the hotel. Of course the children enjoyed it. I had less than twenty dollars to spend and you know that don't go far towards supplying the needs of seven persons. I got $3.50 per doz. for chickens, 25 cents for butter 23 and one half for eggs. I meant to have the children's pictures taken but the money gave out sooner than I thought for and it was so dark and rainy too, I did not much care. I am sorry I could not get them to send to Ma but it seems to be impossible for me to have it done. I hope you have your children taken before now. I am very anxious to hear from you and hope I shall tomorrow. I suppose you are intending to go to the Fair at Salem if the weather will only hold out good. I would like to go very well but shall not think of it. Ed is working away clearing up his land and hardly takes time to eat or sleep. Mr. Kirkley's brother's folks came the day we threshed, Sep 24. There is a large family of them. I do not know what they will do yet. Kirkleys are settled down on Camp's place and seem to be doing well. She came and helped me when I had threshers. I only had them to breakfast so it was not so much work. Our crop this year was not much more than enough to pay threshers and harvesters. We had a $30 store bill to settle and he has to buy about twenty bushels of seed wheat for that place on the hill. Ed says, "tell Isaac I have no money for him yet but will let him have half a beef and will turn over the colt and three calves and a cow if we can arrange it to suit." If Isaac wants the beef we will bring it over and they can talk over what else to do then. It is too bad we could not pay him the money for I know he needs it and expects it but we have tried to do the best we could and failed to make it. Now write at once if you have not already and let me know how you are and all about yourself. With much love I remain as ever your sister,

May Lyman.

I had a paper from La Grange last week but no letter from anybody.

MAY'S LETTER TO ALICE OCT. 19 1879

Sunday Evening
Oct. 19 1879

Dear sister—it is very late -I have been reading aloud a rather exciting book that I borrowed and we have read the fire out but as I will have a chance to send this to the office tomorrow I must write a little. I received your Postal Card last evening. Am sorry you have been looking for us to come and been disappointed so much. But Ed is so dreadfully busy he says he don't see how he can come at all. He just finished the first sowing on his own place of six acres. He has it fenced in and that much in to wheat. There are between six and eight acres more to clean off and sow But he has to stop now and put in some winter oats on this place first. He says tell Isaac he had better try and come over if he can and see about getting that place of Kirkleys. His brother has moved to Portland and does not want the place and Ed spoke to K and asked him to give Isaac the refusal of it. We were down there today. Kirkley says he cannot afford to take less than $275 for it just as it stands and there would be some more to pay the Railroad before a clear title could be got so that the place would cost in all $455. The R.R. Gives ten years time and interest at 7per. ct. There is about ten acres cleared one acre grubbed, and you know about the house & c., I was up on our place today. It begins to look quite different come to get it fenced & plowed and I like it better than I did. If you could only be neighbors to us that would be so good. The more I hear of Eastern Oregon the more we think that we don't want to risk going there for a few years anyway. I want to come to see you ever so much but you know how hard it is for me to leave home. It seems as if you could come and spend a week with me so much easier. We will meet you at the river any time and take you back so as to save ferriage, can't you come: get Ery's easy wagon and it would not be so hard for you. Ed says he thinks best not to kill that beef until the weather gets cooler and he gets more time. I am too busy to know whether I am well or not but guess we are all as well as common except Jessie, she has been complaining for several days but I guess it is nothing serious. Charlie walks around by chairs and has one tooth. I have school every day. Mrs. Kirkley's two children come up every morning and read and study with the children an hour or two. It takes some of my time but I don't care if they will only learn. I am knitting Isaac's socks now. I have knitted two pair for Ed. I have heard no news from home or anywhere. Now write and tell me when you can come and spend a week again. You know I would gladly come there if I could but I have so many to take or leave it seems as if I can't. Take care of yourself and the babies.

With love to all I am as ever sister May

If you mail a letter to me later than Thursday in the week I would not get it till the next week as we get our mail Friday's

MAY'S LETTER TO STELLA LYMAN DEC 7, 1879 - REMINISCING

Newberg Yamhill co. Oregon
Dec 7. 1879

Dear Sister Stella

Your welcome letter reached me yesterday, after having gone all around Robin Hood's barn, as I judge from the number of post marks on the envelope. That you may know how we all love to get a letter from you. I need only say that dinner was just ready when Ed come in with the mail and the children left their plates to crowd about me while I read your and mother's letters. I am anxious that the children should feel acquainted with you all, and take pains to read all the home letters aloud, and sometimes, as a great treat, I get my letter box down and read over Grandma's letters to them. I have saved every one she ever wrote to us as well as all yours, from the time when you used to print me little notes up to the sheet of well written composition which would do credit to a graduate. I have no doubt you are so much changed that neither Ed or I would recognize you if you should come upon us unaware. Best I love to remember the dear little rosy cheeked girl who came to greet me on my marriage day with a kiss and called me sister May in such a sweet way. I wondered why Ed had never told me more about his little sister, for I thought her so very nice that I have told him many times that I would have married him for the privilege of claiming his mother and sister! How time flies. Now my own little daughter will soon be as old as you was then and I think she resembles you some. And I dread to think that in a few short years my little ones will be grown and out in the world away from me. Freddie is a large boy nearly nine years old and is very dignified and manly. He lives so far from school and neighbors that our children are nearly all the time under home influence and have never yet contracted the evil habits that are so soon learned when boys go to school. They have faults, of course but are generally very good children and so loving and affectionate. They often say that when they are men they are going to Kansas to see Grandma's folks. They are looking forward anxiously for Christmas to come for we have promised them a visit over to Aunties and that is a rare treat with them My sister lives about fourteen miles from here and we have to cross the river, we do not often go. The ferry is not a very safe one especially when the river is high. The diphtheria and scarlet fever is raging all about where my sister is living and we may not go on that account. It is very healthy around here this season so far and we have had pleasant weather for the greater part of the time. I like the climate of Oregon very much. The rains, which to some people seem so objectionable are really not so bad when one becomes accustomed to it, and a few raining days are always sure to be followed by a few warm sunny days and everything seems like spring. We have very little wind here, and never since I have lived here, has there been any sudden change of weather. I notice by reading the papers that Kansas is growing rapidly and becoming an important and wealthy state. I do not wonder for it is a fine country and has many advantages over other countries. I'm glad you have such good Temperance Societies, Such influences are much needed here also. I often wish we could find where we could have better social and religious privileges. But perhaps it will be better soon. We all send you all a Merry Christmas and a Happy New Year. I suppose this will reach you about that time.

HURRICANE

Newberg Yamhill Co. Oregon
Sunday Feb. 1ˢᵗ 1880.

Dear Sister Stella -

Ed came from the Post office yesterday with the bundle of "Christian Union," you so kindly sent and the two copies of "St. Nicholas" for the children and could you have witnessed their joy as they looked over the beautiful pictures I am sure you would have felt paid for the trouble. This has been such a long lonesome winter and they have been shut up in the house so close with the bad weather that the picture and the story books are a perfect god-send.

I have read many of the stories to them and think they are very nice. I shall try to send for the "Youth's Companion" this spring and take "St Nicholas" when the boys get older. I value the "Christian Union" very highly and have quite a large box full of them which I sometimes read over when out of new reading matter. You say you are having a taste of Oregon winter. I am glad to know where our winter went to, for we have had a touch of Kansas weather and in fact all sorts but Oregon. On the 20ᵗʰ of December the weather turned cold and we have not had a fine day since. Cold winds, snow, ice, rain, high winds, in short the weather has been on a rampage for about six weeks. I think we shall appreciate spring time when it does come. You will read in the papers I send you about our hurricane.

We live in a valley between two mountains and are sheltered so that the wind did not strike us quite so hard as in some other parts of the valley. But it gave us a good shake up and scare. There are two barns on this place, one was unroofed completely and the other about half. The roof of our chicken coop also sailed off. The door of our house was blown in and some other light damage done. The air was thick with small twigs, branches, shingles & c. The roar of the falling timber was grand. The trees grow so high here and have so little root that it is not at all strange that the wind made such havoc with them.

Wednesday a.m. You see I have to write letters just as I can get a spare moment and as I will have an opportunity to send this to the office today will try to finish it. I think you are most too bad to draw such a picture of my "little" sister (as I always call you, for I cannot think of you as grown up) and if it is a correct one (and I have my own opinion about that, too) I think mother had better send you to Barnum! Now if you want to prove the truthfulness of your pen-picture just send us your photo. I was reading the "Christian Unions" last evening and in the young folks department discovered the origin of the Society you say you are going to join. It is indeed a very sensible idea and you will probably be benefited by so doing. Do you intend to teach school? I wish we had you for our teacher. Our little neighborhood is going to build a house and start a school this summer as there is none nearer than two miles and since the big wind the roads between here and the school house are so filled with big trees that no one can get there. "It is an ill wind that blows nobody good" and If it gives us a good school I shall be very glad. I take a great deal of pleasure teaching my little ones at home but it takes a good deal of my time and I think it better for them to associate some with others. Yesterday Feb. 3 was Freddie's birthday -nine years old. He is a stout little fellow and a splendid boy to work. I often wonder what I would do without his willing hands to help me. We have all been having a siege of terrible colds and Jessie and Charlie are pretty near sick *today. Charlie is a big baby and has been walking for two months past.*

I intended to write a good long letter to mother but it is near dinner time and I guess I had better send this while I have a chance. Of course I send lots of love to her and all the rest. Please write often for we all enjoy your letters so much ...

MOVE TO YAMHILL

Ed had built a house on the property he bought from Mr. Holston in East Chehalem, Yamhill; and they moved onto the property in the spring of 1880.

Isaac found a place in Woodburn east of Butteville that he was buying and going into cattle. While he was doing that, Alice visited May. They had a lovely time with the children and Alice was ready to have a baby in the summer.

May was pregnant too, but still in the early stages of feeling poorly. Alice helped May in her new house. They were making strawberry jam.

"Alice, it seems that we keep moving. Every time I think we'll be staying, something happens to make us move," May confided to Alice as she cut the tops off the strawberries.

"Yes, I know, now we're going to move too. Isaac wants to do cattle again. Woodburn is a bit farther away but I do want you to come and help me." Alice looked up from washing the jars.

May agreed to come, and started cooking the strawberries and sugar. "The importance is to keep together and getting the children educated. I don't know if I can spare Jessie when she goes to school this fall, she is so good with baby Charley."

"I'm glad Nettie had a baby girl; she waited long enough to start a family," remarked Alice.

"I was so tickled to think that Media named her little girl after Jessie May!," exclaimed May stirring the boiling mixture. "She'll be a year old soon."

"They do grow fast. Lawrence will be starting school too. I wonder how the school is in Woodburn, he might have to go to Hubbard."

Cora woke up from her nap and Alice got her up to play with Frank. Jessie had gone out to play with Lawrence, so when Charley woke up, May had to wash her sticky hands and change him ready to play with the other two.

Alice ladled the hot strawberry mash into the jars and left them to cool before sealing them with wax. They went outside into the late sun and the moist breeze cooled them off. The flowers were bright, nasturtiums, daisies, blue delphinium and love-in-the-mist.

The vegetable garden was tall with chard, beans, beets, and summer squash. The cucumber vines snaked all over. The children always found a cuke hidden under the leaves.

"Look Mama," called Frank. "Green 'cumber!"

"That's beautiful dear," answered May. She looked over to the strawberry patch.

"Jessie, Lawrence, are you finding more strawberries?" The children ran to her with their faces glistening with juice and fingers sticky with strawberries. "Share some with the little ones please," May asked. Their little hands were stretched out ready, except for Charley who had wandered away into the world of dirt and stones. May intercepted the stone before it reached his mouth.

"We don't eat stones, they are only for looking and touching," chided May. "Here have a strawberry." Jessie came to give him the treat.

May and Alice were so intent on the young children they didn't notice that Fred and Eddie had come out of the path that led to the Holstons.

"Hello Auntie Alice!" they chimed in unison.

"Oh, hello yourselves!" Alice turned to greet them.

"Did you have fun playing with William?" who was nine, the same age as Fred. May was glad there were so many neighbors for the children to play with.

"Yes, we pretended to be hunters and caught tigers and lions," described Eddie. "We went out into the cornfield and even stalked elephants."

Fred laughed, "You have a great imagination. We saw some mice and a weasel."

"Isn't that fine," remarked May. The two mothers stood in the garden surveying their lovely children and feeling very happy that God had blessed them with a healthy family.

ALICE'S BABY ANNA, WOODBURN

The next month May was with Alice in Woodburn. Isaac had fetched the doctor from Butteville as soon as Alice went into labor. She gave birth to another girl. The doctor didn't stay very long when everything went well and the cries of the new baby were heard by the rest of the family. Alice and Isaac named her Anna. She was a beautiful baby, and Cora was pleased to be the big sister to help her mama.

Again May was glad for Alice; and Ed was happy for them too. Ed was thinking about the good grain crop that he had that year.

MAY'S LETTER TO ALICE AUGUST 2, 1880- HARVEST TIME

Newberg Yamhill in Oregon,
Monday August 2ⁿᵈ 1880.

Dear sister—

While I sit down for a few minutes rest I will write you a few lines in answer to your letter which I received Saturday. I was expecting to hear that Isaac was sick for he was not really able to work that last week he was here. I hope he will do something and try to get well and take better care of himself. We are all pretty well now. Ed has been harvesting since last Monday. He got the winter oats all cut and shocked last week and this morning commenced on his wheat on his own place. He will keep two cradles going and hurry it up as fast as possible. He thinks with the present force (5 hands) he can get it done in four days.

Since Isaac went away they have had a law suit. Ed and Ed Parrish. Parrish sued him for eighty dollars damage. The suit came off last Wednesday. Ed beat Parrish so he Parrish has about $35 costs to settle. I had to attend the suit. There was a big crowd but nearly every one seemed to be against Parrish and glad that he got beat. I guess he will let us alone now. We went to church yesterday and Maggie Ingalls came home with us and spent the day. She would be real glad to come over to visit you if she could. I like her so much and hope she will stay. I have been so busy all summer. I have not had time to run around any and don't know how any one is getting along. The measles have pretty nearly run out in this part of the country but over the mountain they are raging still. I have not got a chance to secure any fruit at all to put up, have you? I want to get a dozen jars to put up some plums if you will have them to spare. It seems as though we never had so little to eat as this summer. Our garden was a complete failure and apples are too small to use. But I guess we will not starve. Ed saw Kirkley about that wheat and Kirkley says he cannot offer any price for the field as it is. But he will do this: he will harvest and thresh it and allow Isaac what it is worth in the market when threshed, deducting the cost of harvesting and threshing. He says the grain has been very much injured by the hot dry weather and will not yield as much as they thought it would a while ago. It will do to cut next week and as there is not time to get a letter from you before then, If Isaac does not come over or send word to the contrary, he will go on and harvest it. I hope your grain over there will be good. Ed will haul down those boards as soon as he can. I am looking forward, oh so impatiently, to the time when you come and we can leave this hateful place and commence to live more like folks. I am sorry Maria is so poorly; what is the matter with her. I shall be very anxious to hear from you soon to know how Isaac and all the rest are. Is baby teething. I wish I could come over once more but it will not be possible I guess. There is so much to do. Charlie is cutting his stomach teeth as so not very well and quite fretful. What news is there from Colorado. I sent a letter to Media last week.

I have not made my dress yet that Isaac gave me but will try to this week. How did you make yours. I will take those baskets and pay you in chickens when you move over. Perhaps you could sell some baskets to the neighbors here and get some chickens in that way. Our cows lay out so much they are nearly dry. I am afraid our milk and butter will *soon be gone. Ed has sold all our stock but these two cows and thin calves, are going to Portland this fall. I want to go if we have any money after paying up debts...*

Ed had harvested the oats and wheat and stacked the straw. Alice had been dropped off for a visit with May while Isaac and Ed went on to work. This is when something unexpected happened.

May and Alice were having a good visit. Cora was almost 3, Frank was 3 ½, Charles was 1 ½, and baby Anna was wrapped in a blanket napping. May was six months pregnant . The mothers were laughing over their little ones playing hide and seek, when they heard the other children screaming.

The older children; Fred, Eddie, Lawrence and Jessie were out in the field playing house. They were making areas in the stacked straw like rooms, and the boys had a magnifying glass to see the bugs. Just a spark from the straw ignited and started a fire. The children ran screaming to the house. May and Alice looked out and saw the fire take the whole stack in a whoosh and ran out to make sure the children were okay. There was no way stopping the fire and it was lucky the fire wasn't near anything. All they could do was stamp out any spreading sparks around the edge. The mothers were grateful the children weren't hurt.

When Ed and Isaac returned they surveyed the mess and took the magnifying glass from the sad children. They were so sorry and frightened by the experience that they never played in the straw again. Ed didn't punish them because they had already learned their lesson.

1881
MAY'S BABY EDITH, EPIDEMIC

May was soon to have the next baby and she contacted Mrs. Kirkley to come to the house. She brought her 3 year old son John with her. He got along with Frank and Charlie. It was nice to have everyone there and Ed took care of the children. On January 28, 1881, a little girl was born. How wonderful to have another girl; Jessie was very happy to have a sister. They called her Eda.

The older children did their school work and settled into the winter routine. May was just getting back to doing her house work when an epidemic made everyone sick. It was little Charlie who got very sick. May told Ed to get the doctor. The doctor said that Charlie had swollen glands and was fighting a lung infection. If she could keep the fever down and get some broth and liquids into him then he wouldn't get dehydrated. May stayed up nights sponging him and baby Eda with water until the fever left. Jessie helped feed Charlie liquids. He would do anything for Jessie and she made it into a game. The inflammation took over his body and they didn't know if he would die. May was so worried for him and the baby too.

Charlie pulled through all right, and Eda also, but there were extra doctor bills which Ed tried to barter for. He could barely pay the interest on the $400 for the property.

Alice came to visit when the weather warmed up or dried up. It seemed to be constantly raining. She brought Cora with her and Anna now six months. Anna was a little blond blue eyed cherub with a sweet disposition.

June Morse

"Eda's a dark haired beauty," Alice complimented her. Eda was fair skinned and a petite quiet child.

"She is so easy, hardly ever crying, and look, is that a smile?" boasted May.

"They say it's gas at this early age," commented Alice.

Changing the subject May asked her if she had heard from Nettie.

"Yes, she wants me to come to visit her in Kansas and see her daughter Rosalie who is over a year now. They never came to see us in Colorado and I did want Ma to see everything." Alice had a discouraged face. "It's too bad, I don't expect them to ever come here."

"Then you should go to visit them on the train. I know you need a vacation, and the trip would do you good. They would love to see Lawrence, Cora, and Anna," May encouraged her.

Alice agreed, " It would be a great trip; what about you May?" She wondered if it would be at all possible for May to go.

"No I can't go with six children to care for. You'll have to give them my love and hug everybody twice, once for me," May knew the duty she had. Ed was working so hard every day to keep up. Anything she could do to help was an added bonus. They couldn't even afford to go to the coast for a vacation.

"Well, I will remember to write to you and will let you know how everyone is doing," Alice murmured. Isaac arrived and the sisters parted with a hug and a wave.

MAY'S LETTER TO ALICE MAY 1881- UPDATES

.........Yesterday I went down in the afternoon to see Mrs. Kirkley. She is quite poorly but is awaiting anxiously hoping to be better soon. She hires her washing and ironing done and most of her sewing so she ought not to complain. They have not moved yet and will not now until she gets well. She always inquires after you and wishes you success but says you will have to be very careful in keeping transient boarders or half of them will eat and never pay. They tried that kind of business one year. They sold your old "Boss" cow to the dairyman for $40.00 and I see her sometimes. Yesterday morning I was amused to see Kirkley out in the orchard trying to catch "Bally"" He had hard work to get him and it reminded me of old times to see "Bally" shy off and kick up his heels just as Kirkley would almost have his hand on him. Last evening Ed and I went down to church and left the children all home. It is the first time he and I have been out together to church for several years. A minister from California preached a sermon to boys and young men and pointed out in very plan language the result of the evil practices which are so common among boys. I enjoy getting out occasionally to hear something to break the monotony of every day life. Ed is busy all the time when it don't rain, too hard, and earns from $3.50 to $4.50 per day. But it costs so much to feed the team and live even plainly that is hard to get anything for the house. We have to pay interest every three months which is about the same as paying rent. Ed says I and the children can go to the coast during the vacation but I do not think I shall. How nice it will be for you and Nettie to spend your summer together. You must not forget me when you are enjoying yourselves. I shall have our pictures taken soon and send to you to have you remember us. The baby did not take the measles from Eddie, perhaps it was only hives he had but he broke out all over and had a bad cough. Jessie has just come home from school and says to tell Auntie she is learning to write and will write a letter to her sometime. You will see from the papers I sent how we had a little scare from an earthquake two weeks ago. Eastern people have cyclones and floods and we have quakes. Ed saw Mr. Holston Saturday and he gave him five dollars for Isaac's plow which he has. Ed will send it the first time he goes down town. At present he has a job out in this end of town but he will go down in a day or two. Mary Parrish and Henry Livingood were married on her sixteenth birthday and are keeping house on Henry's old place near Newberg. The weather is real cool and it rains just enough to keep everything growing grand. Early garden vegetables are plenty and cheap in market. Cherries and strawberries are coming in but are very dear. I think they come from California. Everyone is preparing for a good time on Decoration Day, May 30th. If it is good weather I shall try to go and take the children. In the mean time I will have to make a suit for Frank, Charlie and the baby as they have nothing to wear. I have made two suits for each of the two big boys and Jessie a dress and cloak and myself a dress besides numerous other garments for ourselves and others. I got me a nice cloak for ten dollars but have no nice dress or hat, only a plain black straw hat like the one you found. Perhaps by next winter I can get one good dress. Well, I have come to the end of my paper and guess I may as well stop. I got your letter yesterday, dated May 4th and am so glad you are all better and in a fair way to get along. Kirkley seems anxious to know if you are going to sell your place. This place is in an agent's hands to sell so I cannot tell how long we may stay here but we shall remain in town if we do sell until the children get some schooling...

ALICE'S TRIP TO KANSAS

Alice and the children went to Baker, Oregon on a stage coach and then on the nearly completed Northern Pacific R.R. They had a delightful trip on the connecting Union Pacific R.R. looking out at the landscape. When they arrived at Kansas City, Theodore and Nettie picked them up in their carriage. Little Rosalie wasn't with them, she was napping at the neighbors.

What a wonderful reunion! Alice and Nettie hugged until tears came. Dora shook hands with Lawrence, and the little girls giggled.

"Nettie meet Cora and Annie my dear daughters," introduced Alice. Nettie gave them each a big hug."This is Lawrence who is six years old," continued Alice. He liked the train but felt it was a long ride.

"He's not too old for a hug too." Nettie reached out and encircled the boy. "Now are you ready for a ride to our place?" She helped them in and showed them a picnic basket.

"Here is something to eat to make the ride quicker." Nettie handed them each a cheese sandwich. The women talked and tried to catch up for all the time past. The little girls fell asleep, and Lawrence looked out the window.

What a delightful visit they had. Rosalie was the sweetest toddler, and the parents doted on her every minute. The little girls got along beautifully with Cora leading them. Alice had been upset with Lawrence on the trip. He didn't mind well and it was hard giving him the attention he needed while taking care of the younger ones. Dora was so good with him showing him his workroom in the tool shed.

Alice asked about Mother Painter and how the family was.

"You know Nettie, that I wanted you all to visit us when we were in Colorado," Alice took her arm. "It's been too long since we've been together. When I was in Oregon, I missed everyone so much; and May moved far enough away that we had to write letters to hear any news. May wanted to come desperately, but couldn't with six children."

Nettie realized that Alice and May had adventures that she would never fully understand and was grateful that at least Alice was there to tell them about their life out west. Alice shared pictures of the family and packed ones to give to May.

On their return trip they took the Union Pacific and stopped in Colorado to visit Media and her family, and also the Chapmans. Uncle Eri's brother Joshua and his family were glad to have them stay. They called Lawrence by his middle name, Fred, named after Isaac's father. They thought Lawrence was too much like their son's name Clarence who was the same age. Fred followed his cousin Clarence around the farm and loved helping him do the chores. He was careful with the animals and enjoyed being outside all day. Alice was thrilled that her son had taken to the farm life and was seriously considering Joshua and Martha's invitation to have him stay there. She told them that she and Isaac would talk it over when she got home.

Alice visited Media for another week. They sat on the porch and Media told of her first born dying the year past at three years old. Alice sympathized with her and said how their little angels would be waiting for them in heaven. Media had her newborn daughter Florence snuggled in her arms. Little Jessie May the namesake of May's daughter was trying to catch the butterflies with Cora and Annie out on the lawn. Annie did mostly crawling until the other two held her hands.

Media was pleased that her little namesake had made May very proud of her daughter Jessie May. Media had always admired May and her adventurous spirit. It was because of May that she was encouraged to marry Ira. Now her parents were living next to them in a house that Ira had built.

Alice and Media were glad to have this special time together and the two mothers watched their children playing. Alice tried to help Media with the house, but she already had a cook preparing supper, so she helped with the children.

On parting, Alice said, "I will tell May the news of your daughter Florence and how wonderful your life is here." Media was grateful for Alice's visit.

"I wish May would be getting ahead in her Oregon life. Give her a hug for me," as they embraced.

When Alice returned to Woodburn, Isaac considered the proposal of Lawrence staying on the farm with the Chapman's in Colorado. It was true that there wasn't much farm work for a little boy on their cattle ranch. Cattle took care of themselves. But with many different animals at the Chapman's it would give him some responsibilities. Clarence was the same age and they got along so well that they decided that he would go the next summer.

MAYS LETTER TO STELLA AUG. 14, 1881- EPIDEMIC

Newberg, Yamhill co. Oregon Sunday, Aug. 14, 1881

Dear Sister Stella—

Your most welcome letter came to hand a day or two since and reminded me that I had not written to you (or in fact to anyone) for a long time. I use to be so fond of writing letters that it was my chief delight; but of late it seems a great task, and I am ashamed to say how often I shirk this duty. I hope you and Mother are charitable enough to believe me when

I say we think of you and speak of you everyday, for it is true. Freddie is learning to write pretty well now and he will have to be the family letter-writer, I guess. Well we are all in pretty good health now, at least we are able to work and eat. During the winter and Spring we had sickness all the time for about four months. A little blue-eyed girl made her appearance in the family circle on the 28th of January, and before I had got well enough to do my work, we were all taken sick with an epidemic that raged throughout the whole county, some called it epileptic, because the horses all had it- and were affected in a similar way. It seemed to affect us worse than any of our neighbors and everyone of us had to give up and go to bed part of the time. The children all coughed dreadfully for several weeks. It settled on Charley's lungs and he had a terrible siege of lung fever and then inflammation of the bowels and kidneys set in and the doctors gave him up and said he could never get well. His brain was affected too. After the doctors gave him up he lay for six days before a change for the better took place. But a good constitution and careful nursing brought him through, after all, and we feel more tender of him than ever for twice has he been carried to the very brink of death and then rallied. He looks delicate yet, and coughs some. I fear his lungs will always be weak. He inherits a tendency to consumption from me. The baby was very sick too when he was and we watched every hour thinking both would go, but she is now as fat and hearty as any six months old baby ever was. We call her Edith- or Eda for short. Eddie named her. The boys, Freddie and Eddie are going to school this summer. School commenced the first of April and they have a six months school with a two week vacation in July. The boys are learning fast and like school. Jessie has to stay at home to help me. She is very fond of her little sister and never complains when she has to tend her. I have so much work to do and am not at all strong that I neglect teaching her as much as I wish to. But she is only six yet and there is time enough for her.

Ed is busy harvesting now but one days work more will finish his. It has been such a rainy summer that grain will be injured considerably. It has been the coolest season I have ever experienced, thus far. Too, we have no such storms here as we read of in other states. It must be dreadful to see a cyclone and much more to be in the path of it.

I am very glad that you have an organ and wish I could hear you play on it. Music adds so much to the happiness of home. I hope we will be able to have an organ some day so if our children have any musical talent it can be developed. The two older boys are good singers and learn a tune very quick. They love music dearly but do not often hear any as we have no musical genius here. What songs are popular now? I have not heard anything that could be called music for so long that I have no idea what they sing now-a-days.

I had a letter from Cousin Media last week. She has two little girls now, Jessie and Florence and buried a little three year old boy last spring. She has an organ and takes lessons. She is a splendid singer. Her mother and youngest brother Willie, and step father live on her husband's place in a nice house he built for rent. Her step-father is a doctor and has a large practice there. How does Ellen like California? What business is her husband engaged in. I think I should like to live in California better than Oregon in many respects. But we shall probably remain here for we find it too true that "rolling stones gather no moss." We have not paid for our place yet but are trying hard by close economy to do so. I would like to live where we could have better educational and social advantages than we have here, but I think in a few years there will be a great improvement in that direction.

205

Ed and I took a trip over in the Chehalem county the last week in May partly to see if the change would not improve our health and if it would pay to sell out here and take a homestead in that valley. But we found such a wild rough country that we come back feeling satisfied to remain here. My sister and her family went to the coast in July and spent three weeks enjoying Old Ocean. Ed says we will go next summer. It is becoming very popular for all classes of people, farmers as well as city folks, to go to the coast for a vacation. It takes about three days to go from here with a team.

Is it not sad how our President is laid on a bed of suffering through all this long hot summer, just on account of a half witted man's passion. And his poor wife how she must suffer with anxiety and fear. It seems as if the whole country suffers with them, but we are thankful to be cheered by the hope of his recovery, though he will probably suffer a long time yet. Well I have written quite a long letter for me. There seems to be so little of interest to write about for we live very quiet uneventful lives.

Your letters are very interesting and very welcome to us. I hope to hear from you often. Give our love to all the dear ones of this family circle. How nice it would be to live where we could see them once in a while. I wish you would send your photo. Perhaps Ed will write some before I send this—good bye for now from Sister May Lyman

Note: President James Garfield was assassinated, suffered over the summer, and died Sept 19,1881

1882
MAY AND ED MOVE TO PORTLAND

Ed sold the Holston place above its cost and bought a place in South Portland. In the spring of 1882 they moved to the house near the old cricket grounds. Ed worked in Portland with his team. They rented a spot to keep their team at a neighboring farm and put the cows out to pasture. Their house had a view of the Willamette River, and was in walking distance to the steamboat landing.

In the fall Fred, Eddie, and Jessie went to school at the Harrison School. A new school was being built and when it was completed they went to that one called the Failing School. May was happy to have the children in school which gave her more time with the young ones.

MAY'S LETTER TO ALICE IN COLORADO, MAY, 1882

Portland, Oregon, May 1882 ..

I read in last night's paper of the death of Mr. Galland of Butteville. He was here in Portland and died very suddenly of heart disease at the residence of Auntie Best, Mrs. Galland's sister. His funeral took place this morning at 11 a.m. here in town but I did not go. Their four boys are all young men now and she is a rich widow. Julius keeps the store at Butteville, Theodore helps him. Adolphus is running a branch store up in Washington Territory and Sammy is attending the

Commercial College here in Portland. Mrs. Price is staying here now. She came to Portland to work out and stayed about three weeks at a place near here and could not stand the work so she will stay with me a while. She has left her husband and intends to go to her brother in California this summer if she can get money enough to go. I feel sorry for her but it seems as though one sees so much trouble in a town like this that there is always some one worse off than the one you pity. Not a day passes that I do not see from one to half a dozen funeral processions go to the Cemetery and yet there is more trouble for the living ones than the dead. We are having lovely weather now and it seems a pity that there should be such troubles in such a beautiful world. I am very busy now days doing some sewing for the neighbors. I pay our milk bill by sewing. The children are just now preparing for a Children's Concert which is to be held the evening of Decoration Day. Jessie, Fred and Eddie belong to the Band of Hope and greatly enjoy the meetings and are learning some nice Temperance songs for the Concert. I think we will all go over to East Portland on Decoration Day to see the ceremonies. I have not seen Mrs. Kirkley for some time. Mrs. Price was there today and says she is well but very busy. Her children are having the Mumps. Jessie had it but the others did not take it. There is to be only four weeks more of school and then a two months vacation. They all look thin and pale and I think ten months steady work in school is too much for children that are not very strong.

They are all doing nicely and will easily pass into higher grades next term. Their Sunday School is to have an excursion to the river up to the Cascades and they are counting on having a fine time. Portland is very lively now and every steamer comes in crowded with immigrants and sight seers. The Northern Pacific R.R. will be done this year and that will be a grand thing for Oregon and Washington. Maggie Ingles has given up the idea of coming to Portland to do dressmaking, and I am inclined to think she will be married this summer. Well, I guess I had better retire and finish this tomorrow. Freddie started to write you a letter a few days since and I will try to have him finish it or write another one. I think you are wise to let Joshua Chapman have Lawrence as it will be better for the boy to be raised on a farm. I find it is very hard indeed to keep boys within bounds in town even when they are going to school and I know with Lawrence's disposition he would soon be unmanageable. But on a farm he will make a useful and helpful boy. I wish I could help you in some way and hope I can some time. Try and take better care of your health and look out for the little girls. Much love to you all and cousin Media and Mrs. Waugh and their families. How is Media now....

1883
HARD TIMES

.......*Ed heard of our long lost stock yesterday and went right after it and brought them home today. They were about seven miles from here over Gibbs mountain. The three-year old heifer has a calf about a month old and Old Cherry had one hid out and they could not drive her. He will go after her tomorrow. They are all very thin. The heifer had been kept up and fed and cared for during the storm which cost him three dollars but he was glad to find them all alive. We will probably have five cows to milk this summer possibly six. A falling limb during the wind storm struck old Doll on the leg and it is somewhat swollen yet but nothing serious I guess. I fear the roads are blocked so we can never go anywhere again. I think of you every minute nearly, and as the time for your sickness draws near I feel sometimes like flying when I think how we have to be separated. But let us hope it will not always be so. Try to think up some way for us to get together and I will do my best to accomplish it. Well, the house is cold and I had better stop. Be sure and let me hear from you every week if possible for it is all I have to look forward to. I shall look for Isaac if there is any hope.*

Love to Maria and hers. I am so glad you have her there. Take good care of your selves. Kiss the rosy cheeked darlings- how thankful I feel that they are well. It seems as if I never knew how I loved them till I thought I might never see them again...

May was concerned about Alice giving birth to her next child and she wasn't very close to help her. She was waiting to hear from Isaac, but when he came by it wasn't the news she expected. Isaac told them that Alice had gone into labor early and he had gone for the doctor. But the baby didn't make it. Somehow the umbilical cord was wrapped around the baby's neck and it was dead at birth.

How sad this made May. She took the little ones and went to visit Alice to console her. How hard it was to lose another little life.

"It's so nice to see you," Alice greeted May and the children. She was resting in bed.

"I had to come and find out how you are doing." May gave Alice a hug while the children went to play. May tucked in Eda for a nap.

Alice told May of their plans.

"We thought we'd go back to Colorado by train. Isaac really liked it there. The dry heat is better for his rheumatism than this wet climate. He has been feeling poorly for a time."

"I'm going to miss you dreadfully, sister," sighed May taking her arm. "We have spent most of our lives together and it's hard to converse by letter. But you must go and be with Isaac and your family." They spent the afternoon reminiscing and finally said their good-byes.

May went back to Portland on the steamboat with her children. Ed was there to meet them.

When May received a letter from Alice in the early summer it wasn't at all good. Isaac had taken a fall. He had broken some ribs and the doctor said his lungs were punctured. He only lasted a few days. Alice and her children were staying with Joshua and Martha Chapman. She didn't know what she would do now. Lawrence was getting along fine since he had made best pals with Clarence

Chapman of the same age the previous summer.

The summer was very hot and humid. Ed kept complaining how hot it was and that plowing and cultivating made the horses so thirsty. He had to stop every now and then for water. One late afternoon Ed came home and went to bed. May could only think it was heat stroke. Ed began to talk in his sleep or sit bolt upright staring as if into nothing. May wiped his forehead with a cool cloth as he was very hot. She felt he had been overworking in the hot sun. By morning he was no better and not talking any sense. May called on the neighbor to get the doctor. When the doctor came he decided to take him to the hospital in East Portland for an evaluation. They declared he had lost his mind.

It was soon after Ed got sick that the children came down with scarlet fever. May was frantic trying to care for them. The baby Edith was the worst, and all the sponge baths couldn't bring her temperature down. She went quickly and May focused on the others until they were well. Edith was buried in August 1883 at the Fir Pioneer Cemetery in Portland. She was two and a half years old.

May kept praying that Ed would get better and visited him when she could arrange for the children to stay with friends.

May's letter to Alice in Colorado, September 1883

......a great relief to my mind to feel that in case I should be sick or die the children will be looked after. I have found so many warm, true hearted Christian people this summer whom I should never have known had I not been in trouble. I do not ask for charity so long as I can earn enough to keep us comfortable. But I will not refuse help that is so kindly and freely offered for the children's sake. I intend to take good care of my health as I know that is my best friend if I want to be independent. In three or four years my boys can make our living and in the meantime it is no disgrace to accept other people's aid for if I were wealthy it would be my greatest pleasure to help those less fortunate. As for my poor husband, there is nothing cheerful to say of him. For the last month there has been no change in him as I see. Physically he never has been so well since I have known him as he is now. He looks fleshier and better color than ever before and seems to feel well, although the physician told me yesterday when I saw him that he has fits of despondency although generally he is in good spirits. I cannot tell you how unutterably sad it is to me to look on him-young, strong, healthy and able to work as hard as any man, yet all he lacks is reasoning power to control himself. It is too dreadful to think how we all need him and he is the most helpless one of us all. The doctors do not give me much encouragement as to his recovery although they have not pronounced him incurable yet. But a few months will decide it. The Asylum at Salem is now completed and the patients will be removed next week. I shall see him once more before he goes. They will have better care up there and will be more comfortable in every way than they are here and this fact reconciles me to his going. In fact it is no comfort to go and see him now. It makes me sick nearly every time I go. But he is always so glad to see me and holds fast to my hand every moment. I have allowed each one of the children to go over once to see him. He missed Eda when I took Charlie and Frank over and asked where she was. When I told him the sad truth he did not seem to realize it at all. I feared it would excite him but it did not. He does not worry about us or his business. I try to keep cheerful and hopeful for the sake of the children. Sometimes the burden seems more than I can bear and I have to fight some hard battles with myself but duty is clear enough and I will try to do it. These children look to me as their sole guide and help now and God grant me strength and wisdom to keep them in the right until they can look out for themselves and me too. As for you, dear sister, how I wish I could lighten your burdens. Perhaps in the spring there will be a change for the better for all of us. Do try and keep well in body as that is the best to help yourself. I would not hesitate to ask Joshua for help and take all the help that you can get. It is no disgrace and will save you much care. Do you know where Rensselaer is? He ought to help you and would, no doubt, if he knew how you are situated. Does Media and Ira help you? I think it would have been better if you had kept your household furniture so you could have a little place to call your home, but you can judge of that better than I....

The facility in Salem was for 400 patients and had much better care. May didn't know how she and the children would manage. She sold the team and cows and put the house up for sale. Friends were very kind to her and eventually the children went to other people to care for so that May could work.

Uncle Eri and Maria Chapman took Frank and Charlie. Jessie went to P.J.Cone in Butteville, Eddie was with Ance Cone. May stayed with Mrs. Galland in Butteville, she had always been so kind to May. Fred stayed in Portland working for "Hinds the Printer."

May could see Jessie and Eddie most every day. Uncle Eri would bring the two younger boys to visit. Eddie contracted an infection and at the advice of Mrs. Galland who was a Jewess, May took Eddie to Portland to see a doctor and have surgery similar to circumcision. They stayed in Portland where May worked for Mrs. Deardorf doing washing, ironing, and clothes alterations and kept an eye on Eddie convalescing.

1884
ED'S RECOVERY

MAY'S LETTER TO MOTHER LYMAN JAN. 24, 1884 WORK

Portland, Or. Jan. 24, 1884 Thursday afternoon.

My dear Mother,

I have not yet received an answer to the last letter I wrote you, but as I have time this afternoon, I will improve it by writing again. As you see from the heading of this letter, I am again in Portland. I left Butteville nearly nearly three weeks ago and came down here to attend to some business matters and also to try and find employment of some kind suited to my strength and ability. It took me a week to arrange the business matters and then I succeeded in securing a place to work and have been here now a little more than a week. You may be surprised at this movement but I think you agree with me that it is better for the present.

As you know there has been no income to keep us going since the first of last July. After the children got well my own health was so poor for two or three months that I was not able to do much work. But I got our winter sewing done, and my health gradually improved, partly owing to the fact that my dear husband was recovering which gave me new life and hope. Early in January the Doctors assured me that he was so well that I might soon look for his return. But I feared if he should come and find us living up the little money we had left he would think it necessary to go right to work hard as ever to endeavor to get back what we had lost. So I talked it over with my dear friend, Mrs. Galland, who has helped me so much by her bright encouraging words and sound judgment. She said if I wanted to be free to go and work she would keep my two little boys and Jessie would remain with Mrs Cone, where she has been over since we first came to Butteville. This would leave me free to go away and see what I can do. I brought Eddie with me in order to consult a good physician and try to get him cured. He has never seemed well since he had the scarlet fever last summer and I was convinced that something ought to be done for him. I talked to the leading surgeon and physician in city who after a thorough examination said he would have to perform a surgical operation on him, but assured me that the boy would be cured in three mouths. I consented for him to treat him. It is now two weeks and one day since he commenced and I can see some improvement in Eddie, but he is still weak and nervous. The disease was kidney and liver complaint and there was considerable inflammation and the spine had become affected and the whole nervous system was impaired, but taking it in time I trust my poor little boy may yet become strong and healthy...He has suffered a great deal and does yet. But he is gaining now. The weather is so beautiful now that I keep him out in the fresh air and give him nourishing food, but not very much medicine.

I secured a position to do light house work and have the privilege of keeping Eddie with me. I get sixteen dollars a month clear of my board. The family consists of a widow lady and one son, a young man who is studying for the ministry and keeps to his room all the time except at meals. The house is large and nicely furnished and everything is conveniently arranged for work. The lady is an invalid and very particular to have things neat and orderly, but of course where the family is so small there is no trouble in keeping things nice. She is very pleasant and kind and so good to Eddie and gives him many things to help him pass away the time while he is confined to the house. Yesterday was the first day he was able to go out for two weeks. I have no washing to do except my own and Eddies and have plenty of leisure time. Freddie came down a few days after I did. I secured a position for him as soon as I could and sent for him. He is employed as a messenger boy in the printing office just the same as he was two years ago. He gets sixteen dollars the first month and twenty the second. He has to board himself out of that but I have arranged so his board will not cost much. He is in a good family and working for a good man who will treat him well. He seems satisfied and glad to be earning something.

Sunday evening. Jan 27, 84

I did not have time to finish this and send by the last mail, so I will endeavor to finish it tonight.

The weather suddenly changed last Thursday night and the ground has been white with snow ever since. It is not cold, however and is rapidly thawing now. This has been a long, dull, lonely day. Fred was here with us most all day. He boards now just across the street from me, and I can see him every day. I suppose you received a letter from Ed not long ago with his picture. He sent me one and I am so glad to see him looking so well, we have so much to be thankful for that he is cured so soon. I have not seen him for about four months, but hope to see him ere long now. I advise him to remain where he is until the Doctors are perfectly willing for him to leave even if he is feeling well enough to be at work. He says now that he intends to go up in Eastern Washington to the new mines that have lately been discovered. The Galland boys are going and have promised to give him a chance with them. Mrs Galland, (my friend in Butteville) has four sons, all grown and all merchants. Two of them are already established in a town not far from the Coeurdalene mines and the other two are going up as soon as they can dispose of their store in Butteville. They are smart active shrewd young men and have plenty of money to make a success of any business they undertake. If they have two stores in that section of the country and that is the present intention, there will be a great deal of freighting and this kind of work that Ed is used to. And he thinks he would feel better to go off and make a new start in a new place.

The Galland boys have also offered to take Freddie up there and give him wages and teach him to be a thorough business man. It will be an excellent opening for Freddie and he is anxious to go. They are good young men, morally, and I would be glad to have them train Fred. I think I shall remain here in Portland and keep the rest of the children here until such time as we think best to do otherwise. If I can earn enough to support myself and younger children, then all Ed can make will be clear gain and we can hope to have a home ere long. As to our little property here in Portland I do not know whether we shall ever get our money out of it or not. Real Estate has fallen in value so much that it is doubtful if we could sell it now for as much as we gave. I shall not attempt to do anything until Ed can come and attend to it himself. I have told the agent to try to sell it as soon as possible, but it is not likely that it will be sold soon. It brings in ten dollars a month rent, which is more than the interest on the mortgage. Well this is a long rambling letter. I hope you will not think I have done wrong. I only do what seems best for him. I want to take all the care on myself so he will feel free to do as he would like to. When my health is soon better, I hope to find some employment more pleasant and profitable than housework, but while my lungs are so weak I cannot teach school or sew. The work here is very light and does not tire me at all. But of course I miss my home and dear children. I cannot be happy away from them and hope soon to be able to have them with or near me. They are well and happy and have the best care but I long for the sound of their voices. This great big nice house seems so dreary to me with no baby feet or voices to brighten it up. I have told Ed all I am doing. He seems not to worry much about anything, but says he hopes soon to be able to help me again. He does not know how sick Eddie has been and I hope the child will be well by the time his father comes to us again. This letter is for you all, for my time for writing is rather limited now. I send much love and hope to hear from you soon.

As ever I remain your Daughter May G. Lyman
Address 65 North Tenth St., Portland, Or.

May had been writing to Ed in Salem and her last letter from the hospital told her Ed was going to be discharged. Imagine her anticipation one day when there was a knock on the door and it was Ed.

"May, I finally found you. Your last letter was from Portland and the neighbors told me you were working here. I stopped earlier to see you." Ed held her in his arms. "I'm glad to be with you, thin but good color." Then seeing Eddie looking on he gave him a hug too.

Mrs. Deardorf came to them with a sour face. "You know you can't stay here. May please get back to work," she ordered. "I'm not running a rooming house."

May's color heightened as her ears were burning. "This is my husband, and he's well now. I shall not stay here any longer." She turned to the door ushering Eddie out. "Stay across the street with Fred and have your supper there. I'll finish things here and be there as soon as I can," taking Ed's arm she guided him through the door.

"I won't be long."

Not finding any work in Portland, Ed went to Butteville where Jessie was staying. He worked doing carpentering to help pay for the children. May decided to rent two more rooms with Fred, and sent for the other children to return to her. May supported them by sewing, doing some nursing work and with what Fred earned. That way Ed got paid for his work.

MAY'S LETTER TO MOTHER LYMAN, MARCH 11, 1884- ED BACK

Address, 64 South Fourth St, Portland, Oregon
March 11, 1884, Tuesday evening

Dear Mother your letter reached me a few days since and it has been some time since I have written, I will take the time now although it is after nine now. When last I was working for a woman and had Eddie with me sick. I do not remember when I wrote, but I stayed there only a little over two weeks, then my husband came from Salem on the last day of January and remained in Portland looking for work two days and not finding any, he went up to Butteville where the children were staying, taking Eddie with him. The day he came from Salem he came to the house where I was working, and inquired for me. I had gone out that afternoon and the woman told him so, and when he asked to leave his valise there until he could find me, or until I should return she rudely refused to allow him to do so and told him to go to a hotel. He left, and had not been gone long when I returned and the woman told me of his arrival and said she did not want her house turned into a boarding house! Perhaps you can imagine my feelings, to think after all he had suffered and been through that he should receive such a greeting as that, and that too, from one who professed to be a Christian and a member of one of the leading churches in town. Burning with indignation, I informed her as calmly as I could that I would not cause her any further trouble , but would get out of her way as soon as possible. She relented at once, and apologized and tried to smooth it over and said he could come and stay and welcome. But my feelings had been wounded too deeply and I told her it would be impossible for me to remain any longer where my husband had been treated so shamefully rude. got supper ready, however, and while so doing Ed came again. He had run across Eddie on the street and came home with him. You can hardly conceive with what feelings I greeted him after so many long months of separation. It seemed almost like the dead come back to life, and to see him looking so well and handsome did me good more than I can tell. I told him that I should leave that place at once and forever, Although he thought best for me not to be too hasty. I sent him across the street where Freddie was boarding and told him to take his supper there and stay until I came. He did so, and soon as I cleaned up the nights work and packed my things I went to him. The woman was very kind and pleasant and has spoken a good word for me to many people, but I can never quite forgive her unkindness on that one occasion. Well I conclude that I would try something else, as I have too much spirit to be treated as most people treat their servants. After Ed and Eddie went up to Butteville, Feb 2nd, I spent a few days in going around to all the leading physicians in town and left my name and address as "nurse for women and children." I have always had a taste for nursing and have done considerable of it among friends and neighbors and was always pretty successful. So I think if I can only get established and acquainted and can stand it, it will pay much better than housework or sewing. I would like teaching school but have not the time and money to prepare myself for teaching. It will take some time to get started at nursing and in the mean time I shall do sewing enough to keep up expenses. I have rented two small rooms in this house, it is just across the street from where I was working, the same house where Fred boarded, and have all my children together again. I rent a sewing machine and can make $.75 or a dollar a day and do my work besides with the children's help. It is two weeks ago today (Feb. 25) that the children came down from Butteville with my house keeping things, and since then we have been living here and it seems more like home. I could not feel satisfied to have the family so broken and scattered about, and now that I have got them together I mean to keep them so even if I have to ask for assistance.

Fred is working in the Telegraph office and getting $20 per month, and with what I can earn I think we can get along. I have an engagement to nurse a woman about the twentieth of this month and will get $15 for staying nine days. I get all the sewing I can do, and occasionally go out a day to do house-cleaning at $1.50 per day. It is better for my health to do house work, as sewing is very hard on me. My health is pretty good and I can endure more than most people think I can for I look so pale and thin that no one seems to think I can stand anything until they let me try. It almost seems to me that I am possessed of superhuman endurance for I never could stand so much hard work and exposure as now. "As thy day so shall thy strength be," is surely verified in my case.

Ed has been working ever since he first went up to Butteville. He stays with the family who kept Jessie ever since last October, and as Charlie and Eddie were there too, while Ed worked a month for the man for no wages. But since the children came down here he has been getting wages. He has been doing carpenter work and thinks he will keep on at that trade now, as it will be better for his health than teaming or farming. He writes me two or three times a week and seems to feel in excellent health and spirits. As soon as spring opens, and he can get money enough to go, he intends to go to Eastern Washington to the new Ceour-da-lene mines that are attracting so many thousands now. He will take along a set of tools for carpenter work and thinks he can do better there than here. I think the change of climate will benefit him. I and the children will remain here until he finds out whether it is best for us all to go. We can make our living here if we keep well, and all that he can make can go towards getting us another start in life. Since his sickness, all we had saved up and worked so hard for has gone and we are almost penniless but that does not worry me now for if we can only keep well, we can soon make it up again. The place we had in town is not sold yet but real estate has declined in value so much that if the mortgage should be foreclosed now there would not be anything left for us. The mortgage was due last month, but nothing has been done yet, and the man who holds it says he will wait three months and give us a chance to sell it. If we could sell it for $1000, we would then have $200 left after paying off, but it would not sell for $1000 now, but may in the course of three months.

The children are all pretty well now. Eddie is much better than he was but is not well yet and still under the doctor's care. His trouble is with his back and kidneys. The operation performed on him was almost the same as circumcision and of course was very painful. His nervous system is affected and he has something like St. Vitus dance though not very bad. The muscles of his face twitch and he is irritable and peevish at times which is not natural for him at all. The doctor assures me that he will out grow it, but advises me to keep him out of school and out doors as much as possible. He wants to work in a store, but I cannot allow him to yet. He helps me in taking care of the house work, running errands, and is quite useful. Jessie and Frankie go to school. The school they attend is just across the street, so it is very convenient.

I had a letter from Ed today and he said his work in Butteville was nearly done and he will come down here to work until he can raise money to go with-----. I want him to be with us and yet I fear the worry and care of the family will be too much for him. The Doctor at the Asylum told me he should be relieved as much as possible from care and anxiety for a long time to come. In my desire to do what is best for him, I lay aside all my own feelings and look forward hopefully to the time when we can once more have a home and be united. It is so much to be grateful for that I feel as though I can never complain again at any hardship.

My heart is so full of thankfulness and joy that I am happy even when I am too tired sometimes to talk. It is fourteen years this month since we joined our lives and I feel as if we are just learning to live now. The experiences of the past year have drawn us nearer and dearer than anything else could have done, and if our lives are spared a few years longer I trust we shall prove that the lesson has not been forgotten. God has dealt very mercifully with us after all, tough sometimes in the darkness I would feel as though He had forsaken me. I believe there is a motive and an objective in it all, and will humbly try to follow the path of duty hereafter believing when I cannot see. You will think I have spent a good deal of time in writing such a long letter, but it is not very often that I feel like writing but when I get started I don't know when to stop.

I never hear from any the rest of the family only through your letters. I am sorry to hear Stella has been sick. Do they live with you, or keep house by themselves. I know you must enjoy having her near you. How I wish Ed could spare the means to come and see you this summer. It would do him so much good. Can't you and father take a trip now that the Northern Pacific is finished. It would not cost so very much.

The clock strikes eleven, the fire is out and I must get to bed. I hope when I next write to have Ed with me to write too. I know your heart is with us in our joy as it has been in our sorrow. Write us often as you can. Love to all and our best wishes for all,

Your Daughter May G. Lyman

I pay seven dollars a month for rent of these two rooms, two dollars and a half a month for a machine and it costs us nearly a dollar a day to live. I don't know whether we will get along or not, but we can try and if we can't the county will have to keep us.

MOVE TO HUBBARD

The Chapmans told them of an old house they could fix up in Hubbard. By the kindness of the Chapmans and what Fred and Eddie could earn during the summer they fixed up the house. Meanwhile Ed had left to a carpentry job at Coeur D'Alene, Washington Ter. He sent money to pay for the place in Hubbard. Ed found several carpentering jobs at various places near Lake Oreille in the spring of 1884. From there he went to Spokane to work with a surveying crew. Then he heard of a job in Bozeman, Montana in the car shops. He went there by rail and worked for a month. When he came home he worked at a nearby ranch and took on a sheep drive going from Oregon to Little Powder River in Montana. He was a man on a mission with renewed vigor. It took several months for the sheep drive therefore it was fall that he returned to Hubbard.

Ed had hoped that the money he sent to May was enough. His carpentry work paid the best. He stayed at home and worked at a farm nearby part of the time and the rest doing carpentry. Now he felt more comfortable at home and wanted to be with the family.

He was talking with May after returning and the evening was cool laden with the damp smells of harvesting.

"I feel better about working and sending you something to get by," Ed remarked. He still felt badly leaving May and being sick for so long.

"It's alright Ed, we have enough. We eat well, and keep warm, although I miss a fireplace. Now that you're here for a while you can see how the children are doing in school. Fred is very proud to help out and Eddie too. They are fine boys. Jessie is such a help to me. I can do my sewing." May assured him that they were doing fine.

"I'm glad that you are resourceful and optimistic. I guess that's why I married you, among other things," Ed intoned.

"Why Ed Lyman, I do believe you are jesting with me." May looked fondly at him. "Now that you're back and all tan and rugged from the sheep drive, you're as spunky as ever."

"The work did me good; a man isn't any use unless he can put in a good day's work." He smiled broadly at May. Then he picked her right up and walked into the bedroom.

Fred, Eddie, Jessie, and Frank went to school with the Chapman children: Fredric-11, Alma-9, Lulu had died with scarlet fever, and Betsy-6. That left May with Charlie who would go the following year. She was happy to have Ed home and was pregnant again. How wonderful to have the family back together. She was sewing some scraps of cloth together to make enough yards to braid a rug. It was quite busy with all the activities the children were into. The Sunday School met every week and May enjoyed helping teach. The church people were very kind and she made many friends. Since she was better educated than most anyone there, they all revered her and asked her opinion on many things. She was a leader in the small town.

1885
15TH WEDDING ANNIVERSARY CELEBRATION

In May 1885 her friends at Hubbard and the Congregational church surprised May and Ed by coming with gifts to celebrate their crystal 15th wedding anniversary. Uncle Eri and Maria had alerted the Kirkleys, the Holstons, and Mrs. Galland to save the date and come to the party.

Ed was amazed as May opened the gifts of glassware, a lovely pitcher, and cut jelly dish and many more. The two of them described their beautiful wedding day and their trip west. Everyone had brought food and had a wonderful time singing while Freddie played the concertina. The children were very happy to get together too, and were playing and running about. May and Ed were truly blessed with many friends.

May could hardly believe that she was turning thirty-five and had all her family and friends together all around. She thanked God for healing Ed and bringing him back to the family.

MAY'S BABY GRACE

They decided to have a vacation at the coast after their baby was born. On July 25, Mable Grace was born, named after God's grace that May believed was theirs. No matter what misfortunes fall, God's saving grace was there to hold them up. The doctor from Butteville told her Grace was the prettiest baby he'd seen and the fastest delivery.

VACATION AT NESTUCCA BAY

May was quick to plan their trip to the coast. Her neighbors, the Bevans, Ezra and Loisa an older couple with two daughters still living at home, Minie-21 and Molly-18, suggested going to Nestucca Bay with them. Their oldest son Silas now 23 had been married a year and they had a baby one month old. This would be perfect May thought. The young mother Mildred and she would be caring for their infants while the older sisters could help with the younger children.

Ed rented a team and wagon; and Ezra used their carriage. It took a few days to get to the shoreline of the Nestucca River. It was a beautiful view of the Pacific Ocean. The beach was long as far as the eye could see, with headlands of rocky outcrops. The river wound around before entering the ocean creating a perfect place to fish. They found a spot with a few trees, scrub brush and grassland to set up camp looking out at the river and the beach behind.

"This is the best fishing here," Ezra told Ed. "Lots of salmon and perch, and areas for clamming." Ed was excited to show the boys what real fishing was.

"Get the fishing gear out and we'll have fish for supper," called Ed. The children trooped off with the men. Jessie went along to watch Charlie. She wanted to catch a small fish. Meanwhile the mothers nursed their babies and bundled them up for a short walk. When they returned they set up a make shift kitchen. No sooner than they could exchange baby talk, everyone trooped back to camp carrying their fish about 15 perch. Ed and Ezra were deep in conversation about the techniques of fishing.

"Look Ma," yelled Eddie, "mine is the biggest." He presented his fish and May noticed that he was completely soaked.

"Did you swim with it before catching it?" She laughed.

"Well," Eddie looked chagrined. "He pulled me in on account of being so big!" His eyes were gleaming with pride.

"There now, I guess we're ready to cook fish," exclaimed May.

Ed eagerly took charge of cooking the fish as the children helped build a fire. He had already showed them how to clean the fish at the river. Fred was really good at filleting them and soon the smell of fresh broiled fish filled the air. It was so tender that it melted in their mouths. This was the best way to enjoy nature. They finished it off with some tea and songs around the campfire.

The next day was sunny and warm. They donned their bathing suits and walked through the grass to the beach. Ed took Gracie to give May both hands to steady herself on the uneven ground. Ezra dropped back to help Loisa as the rest picked their way along. They could see the ocean waves breaking on the hard sand.

May felt exhilarated. "What a lovely breeze!" she inhaled. The salty water giving the air a taste. Ed smiled; he knew how much she loved swimming, but the waves were something unfamiliar. He stood holding Grace as the children tested the water.

"Oh," Jessie moaned, "it's cold!"

The older boys were already in the water trying to jump the waves. Jessie tried to hold Charlie's hand but he pulled away and tried to keep up with Frank. May stood with Jessie until her feet got used to the water. Slowly they both waded out until the waves broke over their knees. Minie and Molly were wading along the edge as their parents stood looking out at the vast ocean. Silias and Mildred with the baby were walking way down the beach. May turned to look at Ed and Gracie, and as she did, a wave toppled her over. She laughed as she rode the swell. The wave was as gentle as the breeze. The sun glistened on the water making little sparkles. Jessie followed her lead and soon they were splashing about. May watched the boys with Charlie jumping over the waves not going out too far. This was a special family time.

Giving Ed a turn swimming, May dried off the best she could and took the sleeping baby. Ed made his way out to the children and was soon lifting Charlie over the waves. Jessie joined her mother.

"What kind of shell is this?" she asked.

"That must be a snail shell called a periwinkle," May answered. "Some shells look the same fresh or salt water."

"What a pretty name, periwinkle," mused Jessie. She went to find more shells. The other girls were picking up shells too.

"What did you find?" catching up to Molly.

"I don't know, it looks like a fan," she replied.

Silas and Mildred had spread a blanket. His parents had walked down the beach to join them. They were enjoying being grandparents. May walked to join them and laid sleeping Gracie on the blanket and covered her with the towel. How nice Ezra and Loisa could be part of their son's family. It was a point of pain knowing her children didn't have their grandparents close enough to visit and be part of their family.

That night as the families settled down and the children were asleep, May couldn't seem to get warm and started a cough. She snuggled up to Ed who was gazing at the stars through the trees. It was a beautiful night, clear with millions of stars shinning down. After a while May warmed up and fell into a fitful sleep broken by coughs.

In the morning her cough was worse and she stayed with baby Grace while the others went to the beach. By the end of the week May was nursing a full blown cough with nasal drainage. The first day traveling back was especially hard bumping along holding Grace. The rest of the trip she rode in the carriage with Ezra and Loisa. Silas gave her his seat next to Mildred and the baby.

Ed was reluctant to leave May to work in Pomeroy, Washington Territory. He noticed that she had a recurrent cough that she didn't seem to shake. However, May knew Ed had to go to work to pay for the house and their livelihood. She put on a brave face and sent him off in good spirits. After all, her children were together and getting schooling. She could do her sewing and Jessie was helpful with Grace.

YOUNG FOLKS

MAY'S LETTER TO ALICE DEC. 14, 1885

Hubbard, Ore. Dec. 14th, 1885

Dear sister and family.

I tried to find time to write to you yesterday but could not, so will try it again this evening. Baby has been sick all day, and Jessie and Alma got supper and are now washing the dishes. The boys are working examples for tomorrow's lessons, Charlie is in bed already, Frank is playing with his top while I am rocking baby with my foot. The weather for several days has been cold and raw but tonight a cold drizzling rain has set in which makes us feel like drawing near the stove. We have no fireplace but I wish we had. Alma and Bessie go to school and stay here most of the time, as it is so far for them to walk from home. The children are making Christmas presents out of card-board and are looking forward hopefully to the "off" days, for little ones. I fear our children will have to enjoy themselves this year without presents for we have never known such hard times as we are going through now. We do not suffer for food or clothing, but have to get along with the least and plainest possible as money is almost unknown. Provisions of all kinds are cheap and we live in an old house that is not worth paying rent for. Ed has been gone now about two months. He has found work most of the time and hopes by spring to earn enough to send for us to come to him. He is now at Pomeroy Washington Ter. Sunday 20 Dec. I was interrupted the other evening by company coming in, and we had company every night during the week. Our house is the common headquarters for all the young folks around, and it is very seldom that we have an evening to ourselves. I don't care so long as they enjoy themselves if it does not make me considerable extra work. The time will come all too soon when our young folks will scatter out in different ways and we will be left alone. My children are my one comfort and pride. When I have them all about me and can aid them in their work or play, I feel quite content even in the midst of poverty and hardship. They are all good singers and we spend many hours in singing the songs they learn in Sunday School and Blue Ribbon Club or sometimes we sing the old pieces you and I used to sing when we were young. Fred has a large four sided concertina that he can play any piece he knows on and Eddie plays well on the harp which he got as a premium for the Youths Companion. They have taken that paper for five years and we all enjoy it so much. I have not much in the house in the way of furniture. I have a White sewing machine which I like better than any kind I ever used. I sewed rags enough last Spring before I was sick to make me a carpet, but have never been able to get it woven yet. I shall try to sew some more this winter so as to have forty yards made before we go away from here. I like to live here well enough if we could only make a living, but Ed thinks he can do so much better where he is that I shall not oppose him in any of his wishes. I have given up all hope of ever having anything ahead, and if we can make a comfortable living it is all I expect. We have not always done even that well, as you remember. The little hand is Jessie's work to you. It is not much like the fat dimpled fists we all love to kiss. She says "tell Auntie I got it made wrong side out but it is too late now to make another." Fred made the card for Annie, and the motto "Love one another" is for Lawrence from Eddie. Annie is to have "Nearer my God to Thee" from Jessie. Jessie has only one card to send with name.....

1886
MOVE TO YAQUINA CITY

Ed finally returned from Pomeroy, Washington Ter. and couldn't wait to tell May of his new plans. As usual he burst into the doorway at Hubbard to find May tucking in baby Grace for the night. The older children were doing school work and Charlie was ready for bed. Ed was glad to be there to tell him a bedtime story. Frank and Jessie gathered around too. His story was about a family that moved to the beach and the children got to go swimming and fishing besides going to school. He made it sound wonderful and soon May was listening too. After saying "good night" to Charlie he came out to confront May who was wondering what was making Ed so happy. A beach vacation is one thing, but living there is another.

Ed explained, "I heard talk on the steamer how a railroad has been completed from Corvallis south of Salem to Newport on the coast. Instead of a two day's journey on a rough road, the tourists were now taking the train, filling the camping area and cabins." He stopped to take a breath.

"That would make it easier to go for a week or two," May interjected.

"Well," Ed went on. "Goods are being shipped out of Newport which save days off the journey to San Francisco instead of going from Portland to San Francisco. There is a construction boom going on to get ready for the summer crowd and to house all the workers for the railroad and for loading freight. They're looking for carpenters!" He smiled and his blue eyes twinkled as he waited for the information to sink in.

May opened her mouth, then shut it. She knew Ed was up to moving, but instead of Pomeroy was it to be Newport?

He answered her quizzical look. "We can move there and I can work and stay at home. You can have the fresh ocean air to breathe." He knew she had been sick during the winter, a cold that seemed to cling to her lungs and had left her with a bad cough. He thought the whole family would love it.

May finally smiled, so this was his great news. "What a wonderful opportunity! The children would love it! There must be a school in town." When the children overheard their mother say "the children would love it" Eddie, Jessie, and Frank appeared. What was happening? A move to the beach?

"Just like Pa's story we would live at the beach?" inquired Eddie not wanting to interrupt his parents talk.

"We could swim every day?" spouted Jessie.

"I want to go fishing." Frank tugged at his father's sleeve.

"Yes, all of those things," nodded Ed. "But it's not summer yet. I'll have to go get the job, set things up for you to come, and find a place to live."

Fred had missed the conversation. He was deep into reading a book and realized that the others had stopped studying and were shouting in the kitchen.

"Yeah! We're moving to the beach," he heard Jessie shout.

"Shush, Jessie, you'll wake up the baby and Charlie," May scolded her. "You can tell him tomorrow. Fred stumbled past Jessie and saw the others smiling and happy about the new prospects.

Ed prepared to go, packing his tools and waiting for his clothes to be washed. May busied herself with the laundry and enjoying the few days they had together.

"I'll get the house ready for sale," she told him, "and list it with the real estate agent." She was amazed at the surge of energy she felt with their plans. At parting she was like a giddy schoolgirl and wouldn't let Ed go without a big hug and kiss. He clung to her and wished he didn't have to leave.

"It won't be long," he assured her. "I love you more than the day we wed." May didn't let him see the little tear of happiness trickle down her face. She buried her head in his collar and told him how much she loved him.

CORVALLIS TO YAQUINA RAILROAD

In 1871 Colonel T. Egenton Hogg for fame and fortune proposed the construction of a railway and port facilities on the Oregon Coast to reduce the cost and time of shipping goods to and from the Willamette Valley and San Francisco instead of using the Columbia River to Portland. This undertaking was quite ambitious and included a number of projects. The first was to build a railroad from Corvallis to Yaquina Bay through the Cascade Mountains. It was to be accomplished by following an old Indian trail along the Marys river to its origin to a location called Summit that was close to the headwaters of Elk River and proceeding to Yaquina Bay. At the Bay there was the need of a terminal, port structures for steamships, a breakwater jetty system to control shoaling, and steamships.

The project was well advertised with its grandest advantages throughout the region and nationally for political and economic advantage. In Oct.1872 Hogg incorporated the project as The Corvallis and Yaquina Bay Railroad Co. and funding for the project got under way. Capital came from bonds, mortgages, land grants, state and federal grants and sale of stocks.

Ground for the railroad was broken in May 1877. Funding, reorganizations and numerous other problems plagued the project but in March 1885 the first train made the connection and by fall wheat was being shipped in quantity.

Source information from *The Yaquina Railroad* by Leslie M Scott,
published in *the Oregons Historical Quarterly,* Volume XVI, March 1915-Dec.1915,
The Ivy Press, Portland Oregon https://archive.org/stream/oregonhistorical16oreguoft#page/228/m

Steamboats *Yaquina City* (above)
and *Yaquina Bay (left)*

While there had been four steamships on this route, one of
them, *Yaquina City,* wrecked on the South Jetty in December
1887, and her replacement, *Yaquina Bay,* was also wrecked
in 1888 on her first trip into the harbor. These wrecks, and
financial difficulties for the railroad, left the route unable to
compete with the better transportation network centered
around Portland. Steamship service to San Francisco ended
in the 1890s.The Company did well until Dec.1887, after that
the Company went slowly into ruin and in 1894 it went into
foreclosure. The north jetty was started to be built in1888
and was extended many times until completed in 1896
which created Nye beach. *Steamboats of Yaquina Bay and
Yaquina River* From Wikipedia www.pdxhistory.com

Ed had already sent a month's worth of wages to May before he was ready for them to come. She closed the house and hoped the sale would be soon. The children were all excited and they loaded their baggage and May's trunk into Uncle Eri's wagon. He was taking them to catch the morning steamboat up the Willamette River to board the train in Corvallis. Ed had told them that it was a lovely ride through the wooded mountains. The trees were so tall that they blocked out the sky. The train followed the rivers for most of the way. Then as it neared the coast, a view of Yaquina River unfolded. The train ran over marshes and coves around the peninsula until it stopped in Yaquina City at the end of the line.

Ed had secured a cottage with a view of Yaquina Bay across to Newport at the mouth of the river. May took Ed's arm as they walked to the cottage. The boys struggled with the bags from the carriage that transported them from the train depot. Jessie was trying to carry Gracie.

"Stop wiggling Gracie!" she ordered. Grace was looking over her shoulder at the boys who were turning around to see the docks.

"It is within walking distance to the beach?" May asked.

"You have to take a small ferry to the south jetty where the beach has been built up," Ed answered her. "There are many cottages around for neighbors," he opened the door. May quickly entered, it was clean and light. However, the wind was whistling around the corner of the cottage. Ed built a fire in the stove and helped the boys bring in the trunk.

"What is said about March?" murmured May. "In like a lion, and out like a lamb." She could make this cottage by the sea as snug as ever and began putting things away until a cough made her stop. She had missed Ed and his sense of humor warming the evening with his stories. He had certainly traveled to many jobs. She appreciated all he did for her and didn't want to complain.

Trains at Corvallis Oregon Yesterday and today

Avery Park, Corvallis 2014.   June Morse in the photo

As the spring turned more pleasant she thought about turning 36 on her birthday. Maybe she would have Marie and Eri to visit with their family. She spent many afternoons sitting outside in the sun and occasionally walking to the docks with Ed where the steamships came to load up with grain and produce from the train.

The family would take the ferry to the south jetty beach and spread a blanket where May would watch the children play in the water, run on the beach, and exclaim at the shells and rocks they found. Little Grace was walking all around gleefully laughing at her freedom.

When they went to Newport they saw the oyster industry and fishing docks where they could buy fresh fish. and a general store. The hotel was very busy and other Inns put up their signs. The older lighthouse building was high on the hill at the point, and the beach front was very small. The cliffs overlooked the ocean.

May was surprised when Jessie baked a birthday cake for her. She was eleven now and very capable in the kitchen. They had some tea to go with the cake and the family made music and sang their favorite songs.

Ed had the doctor come to see May. He gave her some medicine for the cough, but she knew she was going downhill when she coughed up blood. Ed helped her with the cleaning and the boys were always ready to lend a hand. Jessie was good caring for the baby especially since Charlie was seven and didn't want to be babied at all. She loved her school work and always had a little tune to hum and make the chores go easier. May watched her little darlings and felt peaceful inside. She thought how grateful she was to have her family together. That horrible year when Ed was sick and she had to farm out the children was past and Ed was extra industrious to make the household run smoothly. God had been good to her.

"I'm looking forward to Maria and Eri visiting," she told Ed. "They have done so much for us." She was sitting out in the warm air waiting for the children to get back from school.

"It will be nice to see them," Ed agreed. "Maybe they'll have news of Alice." He leaned down and patted May's hand. She was busy sewing. Ever since Alice had moved back to Colorado, May had been lonely. Now He watched her lovely form shrink before his eyes; her small frame wracked by coughing. The doctor had told him maybe a trip to the mountains would do her good. He wanted to try anything to turn her health around for the better. Luckily the thought of Maria and Eri's visit gave her renewed energy. There were still good days. Ed jerked back to the present as Jessie and Frank came running followed by the rest of the brothers walking and laughing.

"How soon will Uncle Eri be here?" Jessie's eyes were all aglow.

May answered. "After this weekend when Herbert gets married. It will take them a couple of days. They probably will accompany their daughter, Isabel, back to Salem after the wedding and spend some time with their grand-children."

"Who's going to come?" Jessie asked.

"Well, not Herbert, nor Emma who has a job. I understand she has a beau courting her now. But Frederic will be here, and Alma, and Bessie." May watched her oldest daughter try to control her excitement. Jessie danced inside the cottage getting up Gracie who had woken from her nap. She cut some apple and shared it with her and the boys.

"No more homework," announced Fred. "There will be a reading at the school of our favorite stories. Eddie's was chosen as one of them," he added.

The end of school brought the final presentation. Already the warmer weather ushered in the early tourists and more workers.

Fred had a job at the hotel in Newport to carry in luggage for the patrons. He did very well making tips.

Fred went inside to get ready to go to the hotel.

"What did you write about Eddie?" May inquired.

"How the railroads are growing, and you can go most anywhere now, especially the beach." Eddie was standing next to May's chair.

"We're very proud of you for getting chosen to read." She straightened his suspenders and patted him on the shoulder.

"I wrote about catching a fish," offered Frank, now nine and trying to be big like his brothers.

"You mean how the fish caught you!" Ed pretended to give him a spank. "Isn't that when you landed in the water?" He teased.

Frank looked at his father and laughed. "I got all wet but I hung on."

Ed was glad to have time with his children and pleased they had some spunk to try new things.

Ed suggested, "Let's go dig for oysters!" The children quickly changed into old clothes and ran to catch up with their father, leaving May wondering if they would remember to come back for supper.

Fred emerged from the cottage sporting a straw hat. "Mother, I'll get something to eat at the hotel for supper, there's lots of food left over after tea time. The tourists are very generous." He gave her a kiss on the cheek and left to catch the ferry to Newport.

Main Street, Newport Or. circa 1885-1895 The Ocean House Hotel
is the last in the distance. Newport Museum *Old Oregon Photos*

THE CHAPMANS VISIT

The time spent with Eri, Marie, and their children was full of fun.
The boys took Frederic fishing. Jessie and the girls went shelling
and swimming. May had long afternoons sitting with Maria and
watching Gracie. The lazy summer days by the water gave them a
sense of timelessness.

"I'm glad to hear that Alice is working at the mercantile shop; she
needs to have people around her." May confided in Maria. "After
Isaac died I worried about her and the children."

Maria looked up from her hand sewing. "Yes it seemed so quick,
and Alice didn't know what to do. Joshua and Martha were there helping with the children until she got the place in town. It was Media's
husband, Ira who set it up." She paused. "Did you know that Media
had another girl? Mabel was born in the fall of last year. She was so

busy with her son Edwin and now she has to care for the baby. I tell you it was a gift that she had Edwin. He's three now, the same age that her first born died. He was named after her mother's husband, Edwin Waugh."

"That's why I haven't heard from Media for a time," May stopped sewing. "She must be quite busy with her children: Jessie May, Florence, Edwin, and now baby Mabel. How sweet Media picked the same name. We were pleased she named Jessie May, now there is Mabel like our Mable Grace. Isn't it strange how things work out." May gazed out at the calm bay reflecting the blue sky with clouds hanging over the land.

"I remember wanting a house of our own like our parents had. Instead we moved so often it seemed like a blur. I was so busy taking care of little ones that I would go wherever the next place was, knowing that it wasn't a permanent home since we would be uprooted again." She sighed and went back to find her stitch. "I'm glad my heavenly home will be with loved ones."

"You can be proud of how well the children have grown, they are fine students, and are helpful to others," assured Maria. "You have given your life for them and your husband. We are so blessed to have had families that love God and try to live a moral life. Besides we can't guess what God's plan is, but we can be prepared when it is revealed."

"When Ed and I have our trip to the mountains, it will be lovely, just the two of us. I'll be getting stronger and Ed loves to travel." May noticed that the late afternoon breeze had picked up and suggested they go back in the cottage.

"Ahoy there," Eri addressed the women as he and Ed appeared from the path. "We hoped you would help us in the kitchen. We're going to have fresh caught fish."

"The children dug some clams too, they need to wash." added

Ed. The eight children wet and muddy had big grins as they came into view carrying their catch for supper. Ed scooped up Gracie as the women entered the cottage.

View across Yaquina Bay 2014 Photo by June Morse

JESSIE AND MAY'S LETTER TO CORA, JUNE 25, 1886

Yaquina City, June 25, 1886

Dear Cora,

I thought I would write a few lines. I have not answered your letter yet but I am going to now. Uncle Erys folks was over here about ten days and Alma Bessie and I had a nice time. We went all over the steamer and it was the first time I was ever on any. We all went down to Newport and had a nice time a gathering shells and rocks that the waves had washed in. We found a few rock oysters in the rocks. We went up to the lighthouse and the sand that was up there was as white and nice. I wish you was over here and we would have a nice time. Fred and Edd has got a little boat and they go out a fishing sometimes and get some fish. Today is baby's birthday. She is one year old. Frank and Charlie is a going to school with Edd. Well, I can't think of anything else so I will close so good bye from Jessie.

Fred is working at a hotel as porter. Ed gets work all the time and has good health. I shall not take any of the children with me to the mountains, they will have to get along without me for a while. I am trying to knit some lace for Annie and Cora but it is slow work when I am so weak. Auntie May.

Yaquina Bay Light house

The Yaquina Bay Lighthouse first shed its light over the harbor entrance to Newport in 1871. It was used until 1874 after a more visible lighthouse was built at Yaquina Head.

Yaquina Head light Station, 1880, Watercolor painting courtesy of Merrie Holbert

MAY'S LETTER TO ALICE, 1886- PRESENTS

Dear Sister-

I know I owe you an apology for my neglect but I have felt so bad for the past three months I have thought or cared for little else but to rest and be quiet. I am slowly growing weaker and thinner and know my life is slipping away all the time in spite of medicine and good care. As a last resort I am going away from here for a few weeks to the mountains.. The Dr. Told Ed this morning I must have a change of air. I have got my family all together now and we are so snug and cozy here I dread to leave but I want to get well if it possible for their sakes. The little box you sent got to us at last. I wrote to the P.M. at Hubbard about it and he sent it. We are all so pleased with the presents. The children are very proud of their handkerchiefs and Jessie's collar is a beauty. For my share too I thank you but do not want you to take your hard earned money for me or mine. I also received the little white dress and skirt for baby but Jessie's dress and cards never came. If we go down on the beach this summer I will be sure to send you something from the grand old ocean. I had such a good visit with Maria when they came over. She saw an ocean steamer for the first time and went all over it. Herbert Chapman is married, only 20 years old. I will try to do better about writing. Give my warmest love to Mrs. Porter and her family. Baby grace is one year old today....

MARY G. LYMAN AT SUMMIT JULY 20, 1886

MARY G. LYMAN at Summit July 20, 1886, died of consumption, Mrs. May G., wife of Ed Lyman of Yaquina, in the 36th year of her age. She leaves a husband and six children to mourn the loss of a kind and loving wife and mother. She was a member of the Congregational Church and by the grace of God rejoiced in the hope of eternal life. At the request of her physician she left her home at Yaquina and went into the mountains, stopping at Summit. But her work on earth was closing. She died in two weeks, away from home and with strangers, but sickness and death brings friends everywhere and here in the mountains friends were not wanting. She received every needed attention and great kindness, the funeral services being conducted by Rev. J.A. Hanna of Corvallis. The entire community in tender sympathy accompanied the bereaved husband and motherless children to the beautiful cemetery near Summit where the remains were laid to rest to await the resurrection of the just and the coming of our Lord.

EPILOGUE

The rest of the family's story is continued through Jessie May Lyman and Burton Pearl Stanhope to my parents and myself who wrote the story from May's letters. Now I will use the information from my Aunt Mable, from family stories, and my own recollection to weave the story even further. This is to be used by the extended family as a reference to their lineage. And for the casual reader it is an answer to what happened to the family.

May was so worried about her brother, but it was the next year 1887 that May's brother Rensselaer did get married to a Swedish girl, Anna. They had seven children over the years. Alice's girls, by 1895, had joined the Chapman family with brother Fred. No Alice.

After May died the burden of caring for the family fell on the eleven year old Jessie May. She left school to stay home with baby Grace and to do the cooking and washing for the family. Soon after May's death, Ed moved his family to California near Palo Alto. He had bought land in Mountain View and cleared it and built a house with the help of his sons calling it "Cozy Nook."

It is here that Jessie May at age 18 met Burton Pearl Stanhope. He had come to California at age 22 with his birth mother Elizabeth Powers, a retired school teacher, to attend Stanford University which had opened in 1890. He started a grain and fuel business. One of Burton's customers was Edmund Lyman of Cozy Nook Farm, Mt. View near Stanford. Burton fell in love with Jessie May; and Ed fell in love with Burton's mother Elizabeth.

Elizabeth Bourne was from Quebec 1852 and was adopted by G.K. and M.A. Powers as a five year old and moved to Vermont. She married at age fifteen, Loron S. Hendrix who had been a Dutch merchant. They had two children, Maie and Burton born in Montgomery, VT. When Loron and Elizabeth divorced in 1871, she had Maie adopted by John and Martha Knight from Quebec. Burton was adopted by his Aunt Elizabeth, Loron's sister, who had married Allen Stanhope. Burton took the name Stanhope. His mother Elizabeth dropped her married name Hendrix and kept her adopted name Powers. There was always a confusion in whether her name was Bourne or Powers, but the explaination by my grandmother made it clear. At age nineteen with both children adopted, Elizabeth attended Massachusetts Normal School. Graduating she taught until moving to California with her son Burton in 1891.

Jessie May Lyman and Burton Pearl Stanhope were married May 16, 1895. Two years later June 22, 1897, Ed Lyman, ten years a widower, married Elizabeth Powers. Jessie May and Burton Stanhope were my Grandparents. I never knew my grandfather because he died when my father was fifteen. Burton was hauling logs out of the woods with a team when he was hit in the head by a log and had a brain hemorrhage.

Their first born Allen Burton was born in Palo Alto and then they moved back to VT and had Raymond, Jessie, and Seth. The family fell on hard times and moved to Lakeville MA. where Donald was born. He died at age two of food poisoning in 1907. Then the family moved to Lyme, Connecticut and my father Robert Hendricks was born June 18, 1909, and a last son Richard two years later.

The family with five sons and one daughter lived at the junction of Four Mile River Road and the Old Boston Post Road. The house was a historical landmark dating back to the Revolutionary War. It was a salt box design with eight rooms and a steep staircase, and large fireplace.

The Stanhopes owned the land with a beach that is now known as Rocky Neck State Park.

Ed Lyman had about ten years of marriage with Elizabeth. After his wife died he sold or gave his farm to his son or sons and went to Connecticut to live with his daughter Jessie May and Burton and their family. He helped them by buying an acre of land across the road from the house. There was a deep well and well sweep on the property dating from Revolutionary War days where they say George Washington stopped since it was on the Old Boston Post Road.

Ed took a trip around the world in 1909 and kept a diary starting Oct 28, 1909 Zamboanza near Borneo. He explored the ports, gave details on cargo, did an inventory of what was loaded in China, and kept an eye on the weather and food. His wanderlust took him to Cairo, Egypt, the Red Sea to the Suez Canal. He traveled on mail boats, tramp steamers, and a four hour cab ride in Ceylon, India. Ed noted his birthday on Nov. 16, sixty-six years with no grey hair yet, while cruising the Indian Ocean. When everyone was down below seasick, he was covered on a deck chair watching the huge swells. He retired at Jessie's in Conn. with his grandchildren. His diaries are at the Berkley University Library along with his son Ed's travels in China as a teacher.

Jessie May ran a tearoom that her sons built out of logs, and a smaller place near to it selling ice cream and soda. The best on the menu was clam chowder and blueberry pie. The large blueberry pie sign that my father painted is hanging in my brother Bob's house. The Well Sweep Tearoom was where my father and mother met.

My mother Mida Steele taught school in Youngstown, Ohio and lived at the family farm in Creston, Ohio. She had met Jessie, Robert's sister, who had married and lived in Ohio. They talked Mida into coming East with them for a visit. On arrival at the

Tearoom, Robert was off from college at M.I.T. and met Mida there. He found out she was the best pie and cake baker; she agreed to stay the summer and work at the Tearoom.

Robert, after graduating from M.I.T., and Mida were married March 31, 1934. They had their first child, Mida Lynn, in Washington State where my father had an engineering job. When that was done they moved to Massachusetts where their son Robert Wilson was born and myself June Roberta. My father worked at the Bethlehem Steel Naval Shipyard and later at Jackson & Moreland in Boston. He designed and built his own fiberglass sailboat for retirement.

I met my husband Tom Morse at Antioch College, Ohio and we raised three children: Tavis Hendricks, Nathaniel Steele, and Evangelyn at the home we designed and built in MA in the middle of the family apple orchard. I am a watercolor artist and he is a businessman. We are now retired in Vermont.

Our son, Nathaniel, his wife Tanya and daughter Nadia live at the homestead in MA. Tavis, his wife Lisa and their four children live close to us in Vermont. The four granddaughters: Kassandra, Madeline, Galadriel and Nadia, with our grandson Aiden keep us energized. Our daughter Evangelyn lives within walking distance to us.

I hope May's Story will inspire others to search their heritage and enlarge the sense of family.

CPSIA information can be obtained at www.ICGtesting.com
Printed in the USA
BVOW05s1543100615

403943BV00001B/5/P